THE MOUNT SINAI MYTH

FORMELY

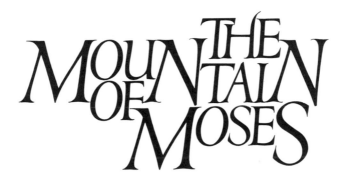

THE MOUNTAIN OF MOSES

THE MOUNT SINAI MYTH

FORMERLY

THE MOUNTAIN OF MOSES

LARRY WILLIAMS

WYNWOOD™ Press
New York, New York

Library of Congress Cataloging-in-Publication Data

Williams, Larry R.
  The mountain of Moses : the discovery of Mount Sinai / Larry Williams.
    p.   cm.
  ISBN 0-922066-45-0 : $18.95
  1. Sinai, Mount (Egypt) 2. Williams, Larry R.—Journeys—Middle East. 3. Bible. O.T.—Antiquities. 4. Middle East—Description and travel. I. Title.
  DS110.5.W64 1990
  939'.48—dc20   90-34638
                                                                    CIP

Copyright © 1990 by Larry Williams
Published by WYNWOOD™ Press
New York, New York
Printed in the United States of America

TO THE INTREPIDS

This book is dedicated to the intrepid souls who break from the mundane, leave the safety of job security, steady income, and the knowledge of where they will sleep tonight—for adventure.

That might be the adventure of starting your own business, going back to school . . . or trekking around the world, attempting to do the impossible.

Anyone can lead a normal life. Intrepids choose to push and pull with history, with preconceived notions, indeed with the universe itself, to discover, to lead life more fully.

We may leave this world broke and penniless, or having acquired wealth beyond our dreams, but our greatest treasures will be the stories we have collected, the friendships we've made, and having been in touch with the incredible rush only adventure can bring.

I want to thank a few of the intrepids who have shown me the way—men like Bob Cornuke, Jim Irwin, Don Shockey, Dave Fasold, Sonny Hale, Dick Ewing, Roy Knuteson, and my business partner, Brian Cloutier, who's put up with collect calls from some pretty strange places, as has Ed Walter, my personal commodity broker. Thanks, guys.

None of this could take place without support staff and people who care enough to stay behind—people like my personal secretary and coordinator, Penny Matrone, who kept the shop open when I was gone, and typist Ethel Warner, who enabled my notes and transcriptions to give birth to this book.

Finally, this book is dedicated to my family members who have each supported me in their own intrepid way. Thanks, Jason, Kelley, Shelly, Paige, Sara, and Carla.

Contents

Foreword

by David Fasold

The red wooden poles, brightly studded with brass, swayed lazily with the billows of black fabric, rolling like a gentle ocean swell overhead.

Through fraying threads, the sunlight pierced the shade within like lasers, dancing ruby light across rich carpets.

I washed my hands in the scented bowl and removed myself from that aroma I had learned to hate. The whole country reeked of mutton, I mused, as I moved towards the rug. Even the back wall of the Bedouin tent wasn't far enough away from the stench.

Removing my abayah, I folded the cloak over me and drew the camel saddle nearer. It fit my head like a socket, and soon the smell of leather brought relief and sleep. Even the women with their giggling, as they entered to remove the great tray, clanging the dallah and cups, did not disturb me.

I was not completely at ease however, for despite the gracious hospitality of Samran, my host, it was a troubled rest. I was not allowed outside my quarters, nor had I been for eight days. I was virtually a prisoner under "tent" arrest.

Even now, Hassan Osman Salti, my translator, was defending my case before the Sharif of Tabuk, rightfully objecting to the claim of Abu Colet, prosecutor for the king, that I was robbing Saudi Arabia of its wealth from antiquity. I had removed nothing, only uncovered a cache of history and, clearly to all those present, discovered an archaeological site of major importance.

Over the past week an embarrassing episode for Abu was coming to light. That is, this was not the first time he had been involved in arresting someone with the same plans to try to reach this site. The year before he had incarcerated Ron Wyatt for seventy-eight days for the same attempt. Abu Colet's position was not altogether unjustified. His claim was that we were spies, not Adventurers of History, and we had chosen to enter Arabia by the window and not the door.

If the portals to exploration of the Arabian wilderness are closed to foreigners today, then Wyatt came over the wall when he crossed the borders of Jordan trying to get to the mountain, yet fully explained his purpose for doing so when arrested. Abu had gone to Wyatt's destination himself, or at any rate had made that claim, and had informed the king by letter that a thorough investigation of the site had turned up nothing.

Now we had discovered something.

Not just one thing, but what appeared to be numerous sites within a small area which suggested, almost with certainty, that Jabal al Lawz was Mount Horeb, the true mount of Moses, receiver of the Torah and patriarch of Judaism.

Any elation over the find was overshadowed by deep concern among those in charge, and by this time all I wanted was to be out of the picture. But Abu was not to be put off so lightly. He had inadvertently made a fool of himself by his early report, or we had made a fool of him, and he perceived the latter. Things were looking bad.

A flash of light startled me as the flap was flung open wide and Abu and his cohorts entered, followed by Samran and

Salti. The message was brief and to the point: all photographs were to remain with them, including the video and notes. I was to forget I had come to Arabia, and forbidden to return or publish my findings. I was to leave immediately for Jedda and a flight back to Istanbul that evening, and the car was waiting. It sounded too good to be true.

Several years later, the story sounded too good to be true to another explorer as well.

Larry Williams had been introduced to me through astronaut James Irwin. Larry had succeeded in gaining permission to fly a search pattern around the mountain by helicopter, the first person allowed to do so. This was pretty impressive considering the Turkish bureaucracy of the 1980s.

Perhaps Larry had the connections to get into Arabia, and if he could, would he be able to get out with photographic evidence? I was sure the area was by now well protected, and maybe Abu Colet was still lurking around. Was Larry afraid to give it a try? . . . Naw! Would I go with him? . . . Well, not exactly, but I'd give him a map! I'd promised not to return or publish my findings. That didn't mean someone else couldn't continue the investigations and then publish "his" findings.

This, then, is Larry's story.

Preface

Many months have now passed since Larry Williams and I journeyed through shimmering waves of heat across the vast parched desert leading into the northern mountains of Saudi Arabia in search of the actual Mount Sinai.

I must say that I have never been so hot, tired, dirty, and uncomfortable in all my life. Those who say that traveling is fun have never driven a small pickup truck over the rutted, dusty roads that lead to a mountain the Bedouins call Jabal Musa, or the Mountain of Moses.

As time goes by, memories of these two trips to Saudi Arabia begin to fade in the struggles and confusion of day-to-day existence. Frequently, however, when I stop to remember those very special times, I realize that our incredible experiences will be indelibly etched upon my mind and heart forever.

I thank my wonderful friend, Larry Williams, for asking me along on so many of these crazy adventures. Together we have retraced the Exodus route in Egypt, searched for Noah's Ark in eastern Turkey, dived into the Red Sea looking for Pharaoh's chariots, and, of course, searched together for the real Mount Sinai.

Larry Williams is a successful businessman with ingenuity and steel determination. However, I will always remember Larry sitting among giggling children in some far-off village as he entertained them for hours with coin tricks. I can still see Larry, sweaty and exhausted, sitting in a sliver of shade among sun-scorched rocks dictating into his tiny tape recorder. And I can still hear Larry saying to me, "Let's see what's on the other side of that rock ridge," when I could not take one more agonizing step.

Thank you, Larry, for a fantastic trip. Thank you for some incredible memories. And thank you for being my friend.

It is with mixed feelings that I think about the possibility that we may have contributed to the discovery of the actual Mount Sinai. That we may have stumbled across the actual Exodus route of the greatest epic event in history is overwhelming.

I do not feel that the writings of the Bible are just good stories covered in dust. I believe that they are events that actually happened, that they are recorded in the Bible to tell of God's might, love, and saving grace to an unbelieving world. As I research the Bible, I find that it is prophetically, historically, and contextually accurate—God's Word breathed upon its pages, historical events that have left their mark on the world for us to uncover.

If we actually did find the real Mount Sinai, I doubt that it will alter the world's view of the Bible. But God has left his fingerprints throughout history—the evidence is there today, for us to find if only we are willing to look.

Bob Cornuke

Introduction

How is it that the world's most well known mountain can become misplaced over history?

It certainly did not become misplaced because of Scripture.

Scripture and most commentaries on the Scriptures, such as *Harper's Bible Commentary*, make it clear that Mount Sinai cannot be found on the Egyptian peninsula.

That excellent reference source says: "The region south and east of Israel, which included Paran, Teman, and southern Edom or Seir, was regarded as sacred by the Israelites throughout the early Biblical period. Horeb, the mountain of God [Mount Sinai], was here."

It does not take an experienced cartographer to determine where this area is. If you consult a map of this region and look south and east of Israel, it is virtually impossible to end up on the Egyptian peninsula. To end up on the Egyptian peninsula you have to go south and west.

In fact, *Harper's*, on page 134 in its commentary on Exodus, drives the point home even further, saying, once Moses killed the Egyptian and fled the country: "Now sought by Pharaoh as a criminal, he flees eastward into the desert and comes to the land of Midian, east of the Gulf of Aqaba, or Elath, in northwestern Arabia."

The Dilemma

Aha! There is the dilemma. How can Mount Sinai possibly be in the Egyptian peninsula when Moses fled to Mount Horeb, or Sinai, in northwestern Arabia?

We don't need just the *Harper's* view of this. You can turn to the actual Scriptures themselves, because we know that on this flight to save his life, Moses went to the land of Midian. His soon-to-be father-in-law was, in fact, "priest of Midian." Virtually every archaeologist I have studied asserts that the Midianites were a culture and force in their own right and lived in the area east of the Gulf of Aqaba, the easterly branch of the Red Sea. The archaeological documentation is convincing that the Midianites were not nomads but, in fact, were a sedentary culture; they didn't move around, they stayed in one place. They stayed in Midian, which is now associated with Saudi Arabia.

What's perplexing is that while one would be extremely hard put to find an archaeologist or Biblical scholar who would agree that Midian is in the Egyptian peninsula, these same people seem willing to place Mount Sinai in that peninsula!

By his own actions, Moses himself made it clear that Midian must be outside Egypt and outside land under Egyptian control. We are told that, in addition to marrying a Midianite and living there, Moses fathered a son, Gershom, whose name means sojourner, or a stranger in a strange land. God himself found Moses not to be in Midian because Exodus 4:19–21 tells us: "The Lord said to Moses in Midian, Go back to Egypt; for all the men who were seeking your life [for killing the Egyptian] are dead.

"And Moses took his wife and his sons and set them on donkeys, and he returned to the land of Egypt; and Moses took the rod of God in his hand.

"And the Lord said to Moses, When you return into Egypt, see that you do before Pharaoh all those miracles and wonders which I have put in your hand; but I will make him stubborn and harden his heart so that he will not let the people go."

The king of Egypt, who was in control of the country when Moses slew the Egyptian, has died, so it is now possible for Moses to go back to Egypt. The mere act of going back fares well with our thesis that Moses had to be outside of Egypt.

That is what the Bible states. Moses would not have been going back to Egypt if he were still in Egypt.

We have two compelling facts here. One: the Bible tells us Moses was in Midian, which is outside Egypt and is, in fact, in Saudi Arabia. Two: the Sinai Peninsula (if that's where Moses was) was under the control of the Egyptian army, so if he were going back from there, he would be going back to his home in Goshen, outside of Cairo, but not going back to the country of Egypt.

Conclusion

The force of this information is compelling. Mount Sinai must be in Midian. Moses must have been outside of Egypt.

Therefore, the traditional Mount Sinais that have floated around the Egyptian peninsula over the last few hundred years cannot be correct. The true mountain of God is in Saudi Arabia.

This argument might not hold up if it were not for what we found halfway between Elot and the Straits of Tiran: Jabal al Lawz, twelve pillars, petroglyphs of a bovine figure that appears Egyptian in nature, boundary markers to set aside the mountain from the plains, camping grounds large enough for the Exodus, and what local Bedouins call the caves of Moses.

We would like to share our journey with you, have you join us in our footsteps across Egypt, into the Sinai Peninsula. Swim with us, if you will, in the Red Sea at the Straits of Tiran at the Gulf of Aqaba. Fly with us into Saudi Arabia, one of the least-visited, most difficult countries in the world to enter. View through our eyes the data and evidence we think suggests that Mount Sinai is in Saudi Arabia. And finally, hike with us to the top of Jabal al Lawz—the true Mount Sinai.

THE MOUNT SINAI MYTH

FORMERLY

THE MOUNTAIN OF MOSES

1.
In the Wilderness
of Sin

Kipling said it: the desert is the loneliest of all places.

And we had just found the loneliest place in desolate Saudi Arabia: a military police compound some 125 kilometers northwest of Tabuk. It was not the compound itself that was lonely, but there's a room there, where we were taken after being arrested and charged with trespassing on a military installation, that was lonely. Very lonely.

The loneliness was brought on not only by the desert wasteland, but by the fact that here Bob Cornuke and I were thousands of miles from home, not in our own country, not able to communicate well in Arabic, the tongue of our captors, and having no idea what would next happen to us.

Our jailing was unusual. Instead of being fingerprinted and photographed, we were courteously requested to remove our shoes and socks and to give a little bow, then told to walk over a dirt floor covered with a piece of scrap carpet crawling with ants. We were directed to sit down and were served a very small cup of the worst possible tasting tea in the world.

All this hospitality was accomplished with machine guns leveled at our bellies. We obliged. After all, who would want to spoil American relationships in Saudi Arabia, let alone anger some trigger-happy nineteen- or twenty-year-old guard?

Indiana Jones and other such adventurers might have thoughts different from mine, but as a father of five children, foremost for me was: what had brought me to this point?

Was it simply a strong conviction that Mount Sinai is not located at the traditional site in the Egyptian Sinai Peninsula as perhaps 98 percent of the world believes despite the fact that absolutely no archaeological evidence of the Exodus has been found in the Sinai Peninsula?

Or was it the adventure, knowing full well that something like this might happen? Or was what really brought us here the knowledge that, if we were able to identify a mountain that fits the primary criteria of Mount Sinai as revealed in the Bible, we would have a strong and compelling religious message to be shared with people throughout the world?

But would such a geographical revelation really matter? After all, if one has strong religious convictions, isn't the significance of the story of Moses, the Exodus, and the burning bush more important than where the actual mountain it occurred upon is located? Or would finding such a mountain cause some religious or philosophical change throughout the world?

This potential religious significance was the real reason for my being there, notwithstanding the excitement. But I enjoy excitement and we had certainly found a bellyful of it in the desert.

Another thought, though, and certainly the one that kept kicking around the most in my mind while we were detained, was: were we going to have to drink more of that horrible-tasting tea?

I knew capital punishment was a real possibility in the Kingdom of Saudi Arabia, but few things could compare to that bitter beverage they politely kept insisting we drink. What were we to do? We certainly wouldn't want to be discourteous. There was that nineteen-year-old kid with the machine gun who encouraged us to drink as much tea as possible. So we drank, and drank!

Most people think Biblical archaeology is a dry and unadventuresome business. They are absolutely correct! The way most Biblical archaeology is conducted *is* terribly boring, about as exciting as watching a potato bake. That is because most Biblical archaeologists do their research by reading books, looking at pictures, and cross-referencing in libraries late at night.

But that is far from what we had done. Bob Cornuke and I had penetrated one of the most difficult countries in the world to enter. Saudi Arabia allows no tourists; you can come in only as a guest of someone in the country, usually to work. We had papers that were certainly good enough to get us in, but much of the equipment and documents we brought with us, if discovered, would keep us in the kingdom for a long, long time.

Introducing Your Intrepid Archaeologists

What an unlikely pair of amateur archaeologists Bob and I made. Bob, who is just pushing forty, has a varied and interesting background. He is one of astronaut Colonel Jim Irwin's closest friends and confidants, and a strong supporter of Jim's High Flight Foundation. A former policeman and S.W.A.T. officer, Bob has been under fire in all sorts of situations in the Los Angeles area, and has arrested more people for more violations and offenses than I ever imagined existed. He could easily fill several books about what happened to him in the line of duty. He is a seasoned explorer, having been on several similar expeditions in the past, and a successful real estate agent in Colorado Springs, where he owns a substantial number of properties and also has a major real estate investment firm.

As this took place I was forty-five years old, a commodity trader of some repute, an author of numerous books on commodity trading, and a former Republican nominee for the United States Senate in the state of Montana, where, as they say, I was "narrowly defeated" on two occasions. Smart people learn to quit after their first loss, but that was not the case with me.

While Bob is basically a cop turned businessman and amateur archaeologist, I am basically a frustrated writer turned businessman. Then I stumbled into Bob, Jim Irwin, and a host of other people who whetted my desire to find out more about the world, and certainly triggered a lot of emotions I felt as a kid growing up in Montana where we dug up ancient Indian graves and spelunked in caves dating back to prehistoric man.

We are not scholars, nor are we attempting to make any representation that we are. What we have put together in this book is our best understanding of what the Bible describes and says should be at the traditional Mount Sinai site.

You might ask, Just how does one get so far out of the mainstream of life, of being a businessman, to get involved in such a wild venture? In my case it happened because a Montana friend, Dick Ewing, had suggested to me that perhaps there was another explanation of where Moses crossed the Red Sea. Prior to this I knew little about the Bible, about as much as many people in America. That is not true of Bob, however. Bob, like Colonel Irwin, has done a great deal of reading, studying, to understand this Book.

First to the Red Sea

Dick Ewing's story to me was that the traditional crossing sites of the Red Sea don't fit for a variety of reasons, which we will demonstrate later. Accordingly, he suggested a trip to photograph where he felt the actual crossing site might be. Based on the lot of evidence Dick presented to me, I felt he had uncovered something and that, perhaps, the Straits of Tiran (also known as the opening of the Gulf of Aqaba) was in fact where Moses crossed.

In February of 1987 a group of us converged upon Egypt to see if Dick had uncovered something noteworthy. It was on this trip, our attempt to make a movie of what we feel is the best site for the Red Sea crossing to have taken place, that I had the good fortune of meeting Jim and Bob. We were detained together under house arrest, so we had time to talk about this and that, a lot about the Bible, and a lot about Biblical archaeology.

Jim was kind enough to give me a copy of a letter written to him by someone who has since become a good friend of mine, David Fasold. Dave, and one of his acquaintances, Ron Wyatt, had penetrated the borders of Saudi Arabia to go to a mountain which, based on the information in Dave's letter, could easily be the true mountain of God. The problem was that Dave, like ourselves, had been apprehended by the police and held in jail for eight days, so he came back empty-handed. While this was Dave's first time in jail in Saudi Arabia, it was Ron's second time, the first time having lasted seventy-eight days.

The long and short of David's letter was: "Here is a fascinating place, but we do not have anything to prove it because all our photographs, maps, notebooks, etc., were confiscated by the Saudi military."

What intrigued me the most on our initial Red Sea expedition was that we did find a place where it appears Moses could have crossed the Red Sea with ease. As you can see from the photos, there is a land bridge at the Straits of Tiran, perhaps a land bridge that Moses and his people might have used to cross the Red Sea.

So it all boiled down to this: based on what was in Fasold's letter, as well as the Red Sea crossing site we found, there was plenty of reason to believe that Mount Sinai was in Saudi Arabia.

Questions About Moses

Should you be a doubting Thomas, and I hope you are, you're obviously going to ask some important questions early on in this book—questions such as what facts we have to suggest that the real Mount Sinai is not in Egypt.

Well the answers are simple and clear. Let me state them to you:

When Moses was first expelled from Goshen, approximately

in the Cairo area of Egypt, he was fleeing for his life. He had killed an Egyptian, and knew Pharaoh's army would be in pursuit of him, so he needed to hide. Now where would he go?

Would he stay in Egypt? Obviously it is not a logical choice, if you are fleeing for your life, to stay within the country of your pursuers.

Another point: the Bible continually refers to Mount Sinai as being *"out of* Egypt." The traditional Mount Sinai site is on the Egyptian peninsula. It is part of Egypt now, just as it was then. In fact, that area was heavily mined for copper and turquoise. The Egyptian army maintained bases there. Hence it does not seem like a place where Moses could have spent forty years with his band of followers.

More interesting, though, is that the archaeological evidence for the current Mount Sinai site is not only scanty—it is simply nonexistent.

If you accept the traditional Bible account about the Exodus, there must have been at least 600,000 Israelites with herds of cattle, sheep, and goats making the trek to Mount Sinai, wherever the real mountain is.

The incredible thing about the claim that Mount Sinai is on the Egyptian peninsula is that to date not one single piece of pottery, nor artifact, nor clothing, nor evidence of trails or campsites of such a gathering have been found.

Many prestigious archaeologists are deeply puzzled by the absence of any evidence of the Exodus appearing in the Sinai Peninsula. Because of this lack of physical evidence, several archaeologists have even taken the view that the Exodus never occurred.

We think, Bob and I, that they looked in the wrong place. If they would look in Saudi Arabia, they would find persuasive evidence of the Exodus having occurred. Most noteworthy would be, of course, the real Mount Sinai.

All of that is pretty heavy thought. To think that we could change not only archaeological understanding of the world, but history. It is that type of thinking that one needs to push him to the point that he ends up tossed in a Moslem-style jail, in the middle of the desert.

It is a bit difficult to say exactly what we were charged with. After all they didn't speak any English and Bob and I speak just enough Arabic to order a glass of water. One of us can say, "Thank you," the other, "You're welcome." One of us can say, "Good morning," the other, "Good night." That's about it.

We did know, though, that the reason we were arrested had something to do with where we were and the fact that we had cameras. Jabal al Lawz, the mountain we found, is in the middle of a military reservation, and it is forbidden to enter. That appeared to be the main reason that we were so politely led into the police encampment.

Then there were the cameras. The Saudis have a real hang-up about cameras. Since there are no tourists visiting Saudi Arabia, cameras are an anomaly to these people. A camera draped around your neck looks to a Saudi about the same as a machine gun would look to you on someone walking down the streets of your hometown.

Here we were, in the middle of a secret military reservation, with cameras. There didn't appear to be many secrets one could hide out there in the desert. First of all, most anything can be photographed with satellite cameras. Second of all, the most sophisticated military equipment we saw, excluding the guns and one radio station, was a 1988 Datsun pickup truck.

Admittedly though, the guns they were pointing at us were real. The bullets and holsters they were wearing also appeared real, and they really were upset with us for being where we were.

Bob and I were not exactly unfamiliar with this type of encounter. We have, however, picked up several things in our travels that have helped us out of tight spots similar to this. One thing is that it doesn't matter where you live, Nigeria or Norway, Kenya or Kentucky, Brazil or the Bronx, there is a general respect and a good amount of esteem given to medical doctors.

Doctors Williams and Cornuke?

Now, neither Bob nor I are doctors.

Nonetheless we do know a little about how to treat the body. Bob has had all sorts of first aid courses as a policeman, and I have studied a good deal about medicine as well. Anyone who is going to be involved in the types of expeditions we seem to get hooked up with better know what to do in case of emergency. We can take care of basic problems and most minor mishaps that could befall someone many miles from professional help.

I took the offensive with our captors, suggesting to them that we were doctors and perhaps we could provide doctoring to their people. That was the reason we were stuck out in the midst of this hot, arid desert—certainly not because we were military spies.

Instantly, everyone in the compound who had come to see the newest arrivals was beset with some sort of malady. Which, of course, presented another problem: how could we treat them?

What I really wanted to do was give them some of their own medicine—more of that tea!

While the flavor of the tea stuck in my craw, and most likely will forever, what stuck in my mind was that there was a good deal of ceremony in the way the tea was presented to us.

First, we were stripped of passports, driver's licenses, car rental papers, all that sort of thing, and then taken to the detention center where two small young boys, no older than seven, poured tea.

The children took great delight in performing this task of pouring, but even more delight in peering at us Americans. After they poured a cup of tea, we would drink it. They would then take our cups, put them in a bucket of water with everyone else's, rinse the cups around, and hand back the cups. You never got the same cup twice. Then the entire process would be repeated.

From this, I deduced that ceremony was important to these

people, so we might as well give them as much ceremony as a prehistoric shaman in our attempt to heal their wounds and minister to their physical ailments.

We conveyed to them that while we were doctors of some sort we did not have our medicinal supplies on us; they were in our truck. I tried to get up to go to the truck for our supplies, but a rifle pointed in my face helped me decide that might not be such a wise idea.

We eventually got the point across that our doctor's bag was in the truck, and they allowed Bob to go to the truck to fetch it. He did this under armed guard and was quick to come back. I wondered for a minute if Bob wouldn't just hop in the truck and drive away, so it was comforting to me, though not to him, to see he had so many friends surrounding him on his trip to our rig. As Bob reappeared in the detention center, little did he know he was about to become the greatest doctor these people had ever seen.

The first complaint came from one of the guards who had ushered us into this delightful setting. He apparently was experiencing eye problems, as near as we could tell. It was no wonder. Though I am certain he was Moslem, it appeared he had had something more to drink than the alkaline desert water. His eyes were terribly bloodshot. It might also have been due to the sun, because these people refuse to wear sunglasses, in this of all places. Bob had an immediate and simple remedy: eye drops. Plop, plop.

There was almost instant and sudden relief in the guard; he blinked his eyes a little bit. I imagine the drops must have stung initially. He blinked again. But then you could almost feel the veins returning to health, causing his eyes to clear and feel better.

He smiled. He beamed. He was very happy! The Great Doctor had treated him and treated him well.

Bob and I now had a full waiting room. Symptoms ranged from headaches to insomnia, sore throats to bad lungs, and a suggestion that implied, perhaps, we were going to have to treat impotence as well. But again, we don't know the language. It was hard to tell. Just something we seemed to pick up on.

Bob next turned his attention to a fellow who apparently had a cold. Bob looked at his tongue, patted him on his back while he coughed, and prescribed the remedy. I told him to stop smoking, which made him laugh and smile, since most everyone in this country smokes. And to make up for the few people who don't smoke, it seems some feel obligated to smoke twice as much. When I made an X sign by crossing my fingers and pointing to the cigarette package, I was met with jeers and laughter. Bob had a better treatment. He told him to drink plenty of water, to get plenty of sleep, and take some of Dr. Bob's special pills.

The special pills were indeed special. They were sleeping pills—strong sleeping pills. Bob also dispensed his special sleeping pills to the next two people, although, of course, they had totally different problems. One fellow complained of headaches. We figured a nap would help him. The next just didn't seem to be feeling very well. He was lethargic, so we thought a good night's sleep would help him as well.

We wished we had enough sleeping pills to give everyone in sight, and wished they all would have taken them, particularly the one remaining armed guard, who was making certain we didn't go anyplace. But the guard was simply unwilling to take our pills. As the others started to doze off, take naps, or become buddy-buddy with us, this Arabic version of Pancho Villa simply wouldn't have any of our medicine.

Another of Dr. Bob's patients showed us a cut and scar on his hand and asked what Bob could do. Unfortunately, in Bob's doctor bag (which in actuality was a simple toiletries kit) we didn't even have a Band-Aid. But Bob did have some Ban roll-on deodorant, which we could tell they had never seen before. So he took the cap off and rolled it across the cut. It seemed to produce almost immediate relief, as evidenced by a great sigh and a good deal of appreciation shown by the man.

The area where we were being detained gets so hot during the day that one of the walls had been cut through for air circulation, and we could see the mesh that held up the stucco. There was a hole about eighteen to twenty inches in diameter, certainly easy enough to crawl through if one had a way to cut through the wire mesh. The hole certainly did its job, providing a refreshing cross breeze to make things a little cooler than you would expect, considering that temperatures must easily have gotten up to 110 or 120 degrees that day.

As a result of our doctoring routine, people took a bit more of a shine to us. It looked like we might be getting out shortly.

Bob had another idea. Disproving the notion that lightning doesn't strike twice in the same place, he again went out to the truck, this time coming back with photographs of his good friend, Colonel James Irwin, the eighth person to walk on the moon, the astronaut you are most familiar with as the first astronaut to drive a vehicle on the moon, in 1971.

Jim has had copies of a photograph of himself on the moon printed up and autographed. Bob started giving these out to our jailers, who by now had brought numerous little children who needed real medical attention. Sadly, there wasn't anything we could do for them, and we wanted to get out. The children were consoled, though, by being given a picture of Jim Irwin, "the man on the moon," and it was clear they were genuinely impressed.

After about two more hours of detention, dispensing free photographs, free medical opinion, and anything else we could to make these people feel better about us, it looked like we were going to be released.

The main policeman, whose name we never did learn, had a .45 Magnum strapped under his right arm and a cartridge belt that contained only five rounds. Neither Bob nor I wanted to try any strong-arm tactics with the fellow. Finally he said we could go to our truck, but someone would take us to a road. That road, they indicated, would be paved. (That would be a relief since we had been chasing around on dirt roads for over twenty-four hours.) It would lead us to where we wanted to go: to either the town of Haql or to Al Bad.

As we were sitting in the truck, one of the Bedouins came

over and saw our Bedouin's scarf and asked about it. I showed it to him; unfortunately, underneath it he saw our cameras with their telephoto lenses.

We had assumed they had seen our cameras, but their behavior now was a revelation. They had the goods on us and everything changed—out came the machine guns and the barked commands, which we interpreted to mean we were to follow the head man to Tabuk, a small community of about 20,000 north and slightly east of Jedda. Up to this point, neither of us had been too worried, but once we realized they were serious and that we were going—along with our cameras and nightscope—to be taken to jail in Tabuk, our suntans quickly faded.

Only twelve hours earlier, at 11:00 P.M., we had left our campsite about a mile north of Jabal al Lawz (the mountain we think presents the preponderance of evidence as the real Mount Sinai) to sneak across an open plain about a half a mile in width (which is guarded by one if not two Bedouins, who apparently spend the night in a pickup truck, back off the road, hidden in a cooley) and entered a fenced-off area where trespassing is strictly prohibited. We had noticed the truck earlier in the afternoon and spotted it again that night with the help of our infrared night telescope.

Although we had apprehensions about using the infrared nightscope, we find it an absolutely phenomenal device, enabling one to see at night just as though it's broad daylight. That's the good news. The bad news is what happens if you get picked up with one of these little gems. After all, they are not widely used in the United States, let alone on a military reservation in Saudi Arabia.

The Night Before the Day in Jail

Nonetheless, the advantages certainly outweighed the disadvantages. The ability to come into this spot to see, without being seen, would be a great help. In our reconnaissance of the area, we noticed that we had three problems on that night's sneak-in. There was a guard at the north end of the canyon, there was a truck parked at the site where on our first trip we had originally entered the canyon at the south end, and there was now a large Bedouin camp right over the road we had thought we would use to enter the area at the base of Mount Sinai.

There was yet another potential problem for anyone wishing to pull off what we were attempting. Shortly inside the fifteen-foot-high barbed wire fence sits a guardhouse, large enough for two or three guards. Apparently they live there, but you just never know which nights they'll be there and which nights they won't. We had hoped they wouldn't be there that night. With the aid of our infrared scope, Bob's S.W.A.T. team experience, and mine as an old Montana Indian hiker, we figured we ought to be able to sneak in, get photographs of what we wanted, and sneak out.

Our revised plan had been simple. Now that we couldn't directly approach the base of the mountain, we would have to climb approximately a thousand feet up and drop into a gully behind the guard vehicles that would lead to a ridge. That ridge would drop us over and down, inside the fenced-off area. Then we would be free to roam around in the area to locate what we wanted.

This was not our first visit to the site. In fact, I would not have wanted to try this activity on the first go-around. You simply have to know where you are going to do something like this. We didn't know the first time but had since learned generally where we wanted to go. We had photographed the area when we climbed the back side of the mountain approximately two weeks earlier, so we knew where most of the interesting archaeological points would be.

The Twelve Pillars of Moses

One of the most compelling reasons to come back to Saudi Arabia (and believe me, one must have a lot of compulsion to come back to this country) is that our friend David Fasold had told us there were twelve pillars, possibly the twelve pillars of Moses, someplace in the fenced-off area. We had not been able to uncover these on our first trip; finding them was one of our main targets. Also, from our photographs taken atop the mountain, we had seen a structure of what was perhaps a temple or an altar. We wanted to measure it and see what it was all about. There were so many unusual points about this site. Things that just shouldn't be there, and we wanted proof-positive pictures. Certainly twelve pillars in front of a mountain in the middle of the Arabian desert is unusual. We were actually to see three things on that night's sneak-in that fit with the Exodus story. To this day, we wonder what really did take place at this site, and why the government of Saudi Arabia has fenced off the area as well as the petroglyphs showing what appears to be the worshiping of bulls and the golden calf.

As the sneak-in began we quickly gained elevation, which makes your heart start to pump faster. Our hearts were already pumping hard, knowing that if we were caught here, even though not yet inside the fence, it would all be over. We would be in jail and who knows for how long. After all, another adventurer who had tried to pull off something similar to this, but never got to the site, served almost eighty days in one of these desert compounds.

Naturally tensions were high, not only regarding our activity that night, but with each other. When your life and freedom are on the line in a situation like this, it makes one think two, three, four, even five times about exactly how to do things, and it was difficult for Bob and me to readily come to the same opinion. Finally, though, we came to an agreement and proceeded to enter, uncover, and document the truth at Jabal al Lawz, perhaps the real Mount Sinai.

But now, after spotting my camera, the guard brandishing the machine gun communicated to us in his best sign language and gestures that we were to follow him to Tabuk, where he would take us to a larger jail and we would be interrogated. The lead guard and his assistant jumped into a beat-up army truck and told us to follow them. What they should have done was split Bob and me up, having one of us ride in the lead truck and one drive our truck. But we were not about to tell them what they should do. After all, we had a great deal of evidence to ditch from our night's journey.

We had to be very careful, not only how we acted, but what we did. At this point, we hadn't slept in well over twenty-four hours, nor had we had anything to eat since the previous night except that tea, so we were getting a little rum-dummy ourselves.

As soon as the lead truck took off we began following it in a leisurely fashion. Almost immediately, the guard stopped his truck, walked back to us, pointed his pistol at my head, then at the speedometer to indicate we must maintain sixty kilometers.

Given the fact that we were not on a paved road, not on any road, not even on a trail, we were just traveling across the desert, I felt that was a little difficult to do. But those were the orders and despite the fact that it was a rented truck, we were determined to do what he said. The choice was simple. It would be easier to keep up with his truck than to keep out of the way of his bullets.

We first got rid of everything that might imply we were spies. We had satellite photographs of the area, which were quickly ditched. We had some great topographical maps of the area; we ditched those. I removed the battery that charges the infrared glasses, and threw it out the window. So now, for all practical purposes, the infrared scope appeared to be a regular set of binoculars that didn't work well. We hoped!

We had several rolls of film and decided to keep one with eight or nine shots I had taken at night. We thought it was important to get that out of the country and decided to risk hiding it on our person or in the truck, so Bob hid the film in a place that we were certain no one would ever look. Frankly, I would not have been worried driving the truck through customs. I thought Bob's hiding place surprising and unique, one that would have worked for any type of contraband material. Score one for his police training.

We also had some rocks we had picked up, rocks from the pillars at the base of our Mount Sinai, and decided they were too hard to get and also too important to discard. These were kept, while some of the other samples went out the window.

It was almost like parting with our children. After being up for so many hours without sleep, having spent a good six hours in a hard climb (not only physically hard, but emotionally stressful because of the tension of that night), getting rid of the things we uncovered was difficult.

We also had behind the seat of the truck two ten-liter plastic jerry cans for holding extra gas. We tried pulling the seat forward to get rid of them. We thought they might look suspicious, too, but were not able to get them out while driving at sixty kilometers an hour! They were too large and we had too much pressure on us from the lead truck to dump something so large. Plus, I was a little worried about what would happen when these things hit the ground. Would they explode in the desert heat? That is something I did not want to find out.

We stripped everything down to the bare essentials, throwing away many things that, in hindsight, we didn't have to, but did, feeling that an ounce of prevention would be worth a pound of cure. We proceeded on the assumption that we would be thoroughly searched, exposing ourselves to additional charges from these people should they find anything they considered questionable.

Eventually we got onto the paved road that heads west out of Tabuk, still traveling at speeds too high for my comfort. But our instructions were to keep as close to the police truck as we could. Along this road we also got rid of other incriminating evidence—finally, even the gas cans. By the time we arrived in Tabuk, we were clean.

Saved by Prayers

The policeman's first intention was to take us to the nearest police station. But when we got there, it was prayer time, so no one answered his knocks on the door. He was a little disgusted at that and I am certain he was beginning to feel the pressures of the day as well.

After all, it had been a tough two-hour drive. The temperature was between 110 and 115 degrees and there was no letup

36

in sight. And now here he was, at a police station that would not open its doors to him.

He got back into his truck, yelling something for which an understanding of Arabic was not necessary: we should follow. So off we went to yet another police station. At that station he got the same response. No answer. These people were in prayer. We knew that, but apparently he didn't. His embarrassment and frustration quickly surfaced and he yelled at us again and directed us in no uncertain terms to follow—guess where we ended up?—right back at the first police station.

We had figured out that prayer would soon be over and someone would answer the door; our time was drawing near. And that indeed is what happened when we returned to the first station.

I had visions of being greeted by someone who looked like a combination of the Incredible Hulk and Godzilla. Big and massive, dirty and ugly. Instead, we were greeted by two boys, one pushing fourteen years of age. The other I took to be his younger brother, perhaps nine.

We were led into their version of a holding tank, which was almost a repetition of our desert cell. This one was a little fancier, though. While it had a similar Arabic rug, it had comfortable pillows along the side of the room, which measured about twenty feet by thirty feet. On the south wall, at the top of the room, were five large photographs showing the kings and princes of the country. One of them was the pretend sponsor from our first trip. The room contained no chairs, no tables.

Bob kept pointing to the picture, telling the guard that that was the prince who issued the papers to get us into the country. But neither our old nor our new guards were buying.

We again were offered and served tea by the youngest boy. This tea was not quite as bad as the earlier desert brew, but it was not much better. I asked the fourteen-year-old if he understood English. He gave the impression that he did, but when I started talking, it became clear that he did not know much more than "hello" and "bye-bye."

We tried to explain our problem and, while we were given

smiles and nods, there was no communication, so we decided the best strategy we could have at this point was to just let them relax. They weren't as frustrated as we were, so I lay back and took a nap.

After about ten or twelve minutes, I awoke. Bob was chattering with them. There was something he wanted to get out of his car. As he got up, the policeman with the gun also arose and motioned him to get down.

Bob got down but later got up again. The policeman got back up. I could see this was going nowhere.

There wasn't anything we could do. We could not communicate that we had done no wrong, although we tried to tell the younger policeman what had happened. I think he got the gist of the story but we still were not allowed to leave. We were in a holding tank, and it looked like they were going to hold us for a long time.

Finally, I had an idea. Like in an old Bugs Bunny cartoon, a light bulb went on in my mind. The employees at the hotel where we had stayed spoke English. Why not give them a call, explain our situation, and have them translate our way out of this predicament to the two not-so-friendly policemen? I began looking for a telephone.

This itself seemed so strange. We were so far from our culture, yet only a phone call away from help. I wondered: in Saudi Arabia did prisoners get one phone call just as in America? The room itself did not look like a room that should have a telephone. After all, the rug was covering a dirt floor, there was but one light bulb hanging by a frayed cord from the top of the room, and a fan (and a well-appreciated fan at that) rotating off center, also suspended in midair by frayed cords. The room was painted in what, back home, we would call a wainscot. That is, the lower four feet were painted in a dark reddish color, the next eight feet a light green. Over this someone had taken a paint roller with a pattern and run lines up and down in some type of mosaic spatter.

Initially I whiled away my time by showing some magic tricks to the youngest boy. It got his and even the Bedouin policeman's attention. They watched with a bit of amazement, and it gave me some pleasure to see that my eighth-grade magic show tricks worked with these people. I did one where you make pieces of paper disappear from your fingers, as well as a couple of coin-disappearing tricks that they seemed to like a lot—I must have made the same coin disappear thirty times that afternoon.

I asked for a phone book after communicating that I wanted to make a phone call.

Even in Saudi Arabia, believe it or not, they have the Yellow Pages. I let my fingers do the walking, but it wasn't much use because their Yellow Pages were of course in Arabic, not English. It was back to square one. What could we do now?

There was a picture of a hotel in the Yellow Pages—not our hotel, not even in the town we were in—but what the heck, maybe someone there could speak English. I called. They answered—in Arabic. Again, we were out of luck.

What's more, the red telephone they let me use was inoperable most of the time. The only way to get it to work was to knock on it two or three times real hard to get a dial tone.

Finally, we had the idea of getting our rental papers out of the car and calling the car rental office to see if they could help. Bob again got up to get the papers. By now our armed guard was in a little better mood. I think he realized Bob was not going to make a run for it, leaving me stuck in the room.

Bob came back with our rental papers and handed them to me, but the young guard now demanded them. I was reluctant to give them to him. At this point, Bob went to the bathroom. I wished he hadn't. I wished he had been there to see me explode at both guards when they asked for the papers. I don't think they understood a word of what I was saying but they realized I was very upset with them.

Up to this point, my role had been to be as nice as possible, to show that I was a man of good intentions, but I thought it was time to show them I'd had enough.

I refused to give the papers to them. I told them I had been held up by them for almost eight hours now, I was sick and tired of the way we were treated, and that our cameras contained pictures of camels and they could go develop the film and see for themselves. I told them we did not know we were on a military reservation. I told them I did not know cameras were not allowed on a military reservation, both points true. I told them by forcing us to drive at high speeds in the desert we had probably ruined the truck and we would have to pay a substantial penalty when we turned the rental truck in. That was also true. I told them we hadn't eaten for a long time, and that was painfully true, our last meal having been about eight the previous evening. It was now about three in the afternoon. I also told them I didn't want any more of that damned tea!

I played this role as well as I could, acting indignant while making certain I stayed centered, not getting truly emotional. I had to stay in control.

Bob came back to the room and I informed him of what I had done. Clearly they understood my meaning; my intentions had been communicated, and now they chattered to each other, finally letting us keep the car papers, and thus giving us the opportunity to call the car agency. I called two or three times; there was no answer. Finally, on the next try, I got through, and decided not to ask them for help but instead asked for the phone number of our hotel, which they gladly provided.

I then called the hotel and spoke with the general manager, telling him what our problem was. He did a remarkable job for us in talking to both of the Bedouins, telling them our side of the story, telling them we wanted our cameras, and we wanted our freedom.

We worked out a bit of an exchange. The exchange would be that they would take us out of the police station to the hotel, where we would stay with the Bedouin cop chaperoning.

Our strategy was that we could do more negotiations at the hotel. The Bedouin who had brought us in from the desert did not seem to be receptive to the idea, but nonetheless went along with it. He watched very carefully as we picked up our things. He would not give us our passports or our cameras, again instructing us to follow him. We were forced out of the police station, at gun point, ahead of him, with his hawklike eyes making certain we did not make any hasty escape.

The thought of trying to escape never even crossed my mind and didn't come to Bob either. After all, where would we go? Into the desert? How would we get across the border into Jordan or into Israel? What a stupid thing it would be to try to run, at least in daylight. At night we might be able to get some distance, but we would still have to travel almost 150 miles to the nearest border. And running would be an admission of guilt.

The drive to our hotel was almost uneventful. We were not positive we were headed for our hotel but hoped that our guards would stick to what seemed to be the agreement. What worried us was that we drove up to the major prison in Tabuk. The prison had walls at least forty feet high with guardhouses at all corners and lots of barbed wire running across the top. We were still following our friendly Bedouin cop when we saw the prison. In the next thirty seconds my mind fast-forwarded the movie *Midnight Express*.

There is a stoplight right at the prison. Our guard pulled up to the light. My eyes fervently looked to see if he turned on his left-hand turn signal. Happily, there were no blinking lights on the left side of his truck, but I was only partially relieved, since this kamikaze did not always use his signal lights. Once the light turned green, he pulled away and continued driving up the road toward our hotel. Our prayers were answered.

Serious Negotiations

Upon arriving at the hotel we went into the general manager's office and the negotiations began in earnest. We would say something in English, the policeman would say something in Arabic, and the general manager would speak in Arabic, then English. Back and forth, round and round it went.

It was an awkward, yet interesting, situation. You know you are being represented by someone, but you don't know what he is saying about you. Come to think of it, this hotel manager didn't know much about us except that we had stayed at the hotel once before, paid our bill, and had been friendly to him and all the people in his employ. Had we tipped enough? I wondered.

Finally, the general manager said he had reached a point where the policeman was willing to let us go, but the Bedouin would keep the cameras.

That represented a real problem. Our camera equipment probably had a combined value of $3,000 or $4,000, and Bob's camera was on a loan from a friend in Colorado Springs. That simply wouldn't do. I was willing to give up my camera if we could keep Bob's camera and we could get the heck out of there. But we thought it would be best to negotiate further.

This time we entered directly into the negotiations, and got to the point of yelling back and forth. We'd yell at the Bedouin and he would yell at us. This was getting to be fun.

Bob and I looked at each other and decided it was time to bring out the heavy artillery. The letter from our sponsor for our initial trip—a bogus letter, I might add, that had been prepared by our friend Dimitrie in London. This letter purported to show that the king had invited us into the country. Keep in mind there are many princes but only one king in this country. He is Allah's right hand, the man you do not want to cross.

Bob was reluctant to present the letter because what if they called the king? He would have no knowledge of us. But I figured that even if they called the king and the letter was real, he wouldn't remember writing or authorizing the letter, because there are so many servants and people between the king and any communication. On that basis, we decided to present the letter. It caught the attention of the hotel manager; he sat right up.

He was impressed. To him, of course, it seemed to be a real letter. So he, too, started shouting at the Bedouin. What he explained later was that he told the Bedouin that the king would be very upset to find we had been treated that way and the king would tell the Bedouin's commander about the way we were treated. There was a good chance the Bedouin would lose his job.

Almost instantaneously, the tone of the conversation changed. Although we still could not understand any of what was being said, we could certainly understand the tone; no translation was needed, the Bedouin was now back-pedaling.

Finally, the hotel manager leaned over to me and said, "I would suggest that you invite everyone to have a glass of orange juice."

I said, "Oh sure, gladly!"

He said also, "I am going to scold you very hard. Don't take it personally; I'm just doing this for show for the Bedouin." He then proceeded to talk harshly to me: yelling and swearing, ranting and raving, explaining that we were never to bring cameras into the area again. If we did, this Bedouin would handcuff us and throw us into jail for the rest of our lives. When he was through with his spiel, he winked at us and said, "Pretend you are very sincere about hearing this."

Did we look sincere—right out of a Norman Rockwell painting.

That seemed to make the final impression on the Bedouin, who then relented to the point that he gave back both of the cameras and let us go free.

The orange juice was then delivered. While we were drinking the juice, the Bedouin told us (with excellent motions that would win any game of charades) that if we ever came back into his area, we would be handcuffed. He used the word *kalibush,* crossed his fists in front of us, and showed he couldn't pull them apart. He shook his finger at us and said all sorts of things in Arabic. Again, even though we could not translate, we certainly got the message, which was: "Don't bring cameras into this country. Don't let me see you again. If I see you again I will put you in jail and throw away the key."

It was certain that if we ever got caught again, it would take more than my cheap magic tricks and Bob's doctoring to get us out of the country.

We kept telling everyone throughout the day that we were not upset by what had happened. We were certain that in the land of Allah we would be treated well, as we were guests of the country. This tactic worked. At the end, we told the cop we had no hard feelings, we realized he was just doing his job, and he should come see us if he ever got to America and we'd take him to Disneyland. And we would.

The Bedouin and his sidekick finally left, leaving us in the hotel. It was now about five in the afternoon. Since Bob and I had been up, nonstop, for thirty-eight hours, we were sweaty, dirty, smelly, hungry, and exhausted. We told the hotel manager we wanted a room, and he graciously accommodated us. We carried our gear up, showered, ordered six more glasses of fresh-squeezed orange juice and then lay on the beds, taking a twenty-minute nap.

Although there were other sites and other things to see in Saudi Arabia that I knew would further substantiate our findings regarding the footsteps of Moses (one definitely needs to return to Al Bad, as well as investigate two other mountains), we decided that Lady Luck had been good to us and we didn't want to push her any further.

For sure, if we were caught again, the hotel manager would not come to our aid. So what choice did we have? Stay in Tabuk for a couple days, sitting in a hotel getting suntans that would make George Hamilton envious? Or should we head for home? It was an easy choice; we decided to get back to reality as soon as possible.

Accordingly, we cleaned out our truck, went downtown and bought airline tickets, and by 8:55 P.M. were checked through the Jedda airport. Here the passport paper trip began.

Homeward Bound

Before we were out of the country we had to show our passports and have our luggage checked seven times.

Landing in Riyadh was a real experience. As we walked into Riyadh's big-time, cosmopolitan airport we were taken aback by its cleanliness and freshness. The only thing missing was a Nordstrom's or some other large department store. It gave the feeling of being in the Water Place Tower in Chicago, or even Trump Tower in New York. Although it was a beautiful airport, there were no shops to speak of, not even a decent place to eat. But that was hardly our greatest concern. Our concern was just getting on a plane, out of the country, on our way to New York.

The last leg of our flight to New York provides a little asterisk to this entire escapade. By this time we had not had any serious sleep for about fifty hours. We'd been up the night before till three and the night before that in London until five, watching the Tyson-Spinks fight.

Before boarding the plane, we each took one of Bob's sleeping pills, a great way to get through a fourteen-hour flight. By the time the plane was wheels-up, Bob had talked the man sitting between the two of us into sitting in another seat. That way Bob could lie down across three seats. I blew up my air mattress, and lay on the floor of the airplane sprawled between seat supports. With foul-tasting snacks in our bellies from the airport we were as well fed as one could expect. Exactly thirteen hours later we both awoke.

I think the longest I had ever slept in an airplane before was four hours. The longest I ever heard of anyone else sleeping in a plane is six hours. Thirteen hours! I think that sets a world record.

People talk about falling asleep, but I didn't really fall asleep on the trip back. Falling asleep implies moving into a different position, as in falling off a log or falling out of a tree. It was more that sleep just overcame my entire body. In that process, a fascinating thing occurred.

I vividly recall that as sleep was starting to wrap its wonderful blankets around my body, my mind replayed many of the things that had occurred in the last thirty-six hours. Interestingly enough, everything, the visions, that motion picture inside my mind, was in infrared green, just as though I were still looking through our nightscope. But what I saw was also different from what had taken place that day. I saw that we had done something no one else had ever done. We had gotten into and out of Saudi Arabia with concrete evidence about what may well be a major archaeological find.

I could clearly see and replay our trip up the mountain, seeing the cave that's on the mountain, which might well be the cave of Elijah. This is significant, because on the other alleged Mount Sinais, there are no caves. On this point, the Bible is very clear. Elijah went to Mount Sinai to spend forty days inside a cave. Thus, wherever the true Mount Sinai is, there must be a cave. Only Jabal al Lawz has a cave.

And then there were those twelve pillars. They kept popping into my mind, taking on all sorts of different shapes from what they actually were. But they were still there, pillars, or rings, or whatever you want to call them, at the base of the mountain. No one has ever found twelve pillars—the twelve pillars of Moses?—at any of the other proposed Mount Sinais.

And then my mind's eye turned to the Biblical text.

One of the unusual things about my sleeping habits is that I go to sleep at night seeing book pages in my mind. While other people may count sheep, I see books. I don't know what those books are or where they are from, but there is book print or newsprint in front of me. What came up in the airplane were Biblical writings, mostly from Exodus and Numbers. And in every instance they consistently fit with the terrain and physical attributes of Jabal al Lawz.

Just before sleep totally engulfed my body, there was a warm feeling, a sense of accomplishment not only of getting in and out of the country, not only in getting photographs of hard evidence, but a sense of awareness that we might have made a major archaeological find that would have political and religious implications for years to come. Whether or not that is correct remains to be seen. But now we would like to present to you, dear reader, the hard evidence that we found at the mountain, as well as the Biblical references we think definitely indi-

46

cate that Mount Sinai is not where most people think it is but is, in fact, in Saudi Arabia.

In the rest of this book we are going to open your eyes to an entirely new way of looking at Exodus and give you a clearer understanding of this great Biblical story than you have ever had before. Travel with us now . . .

2.
Out of Egypt

It's not just in Exodus that we get the feeling that Moses was not in Egypt. The same refrain is repeated in Jeremiah 7:22. God himself spoke, saying in reference to Moses: "For in the day that I brought them out of the land of Egypt. . . ."

If you study the archaeological or scholarly Biblical literature written over the years regarding the true Mount Sinai, you will find there simply is no agreement as to where it is located. This is amazing. Even such probing scholars as Umberto Cassuto, writing in 1988 in *A Commentary of the Book of Exodus*, states: "It is still impossible to determine precisely the site of the Biblical Mount Sinai."

See for yourself. Turn to the back of any Bible that has maps and look at the one of the Sinai Peninsula. Then look at Mount Sinai. There, in just about every Bible, you'll see Mount Sinai labeled—with a question mark next to it.

Yet if you consult the average person on the streets of Tel Aviv you'll find he's totally convinced he knows where Mount Sinai is; and if you ask a tourist on a bus in Cairo, you'll find *him* totally convinced he is on his way to the one and only Mount Sinai.

The myth of the real Mount Sinai being at the southernmost tip of the Sinai Peninsula in Egypt has been propagated actively now for almost 250 years. Prior to that time, numerous other mountains were claimed to be the real thing. In fact, we have found six major reasons all strongly suggesting that the true Mount Sinai cannot in any way be located where the public and tourists go—to the Monastery of St. Catherine, on the impostor mountain, standing some 8,626 feet above sea level, close to the tip of the Sinai Peninsula.

Professional opinion is sharply divided as to where the true mountain is located, with perhaps 15 percent, or no more than 20 percent, of professional archaeologists and Biblical scholars giving credence to the traditional site. And even those have been put to the test in recent years because of the absence of any documentation of Moses' era at Mount Sinai.

We first must give credit where credit is due. Certainly the traditional Mount Sinai site is majestic, is beautiful, and is awe-inspiring. But that is all it has going for it as being the true Mount Horeb. In fact, it may well be that the traditional site is the longest-running tourist scam in the history of the world. I think you will shortly agree.

Hiding in the Enemy's Camp

In discussions with professional archaeologists and Biblical scholars, there is one point that is the most telling about what is wrong with the current site. It has very little to do with archaeology, Biblical history, Biblical sites, or possible Biblical sites.

It is conjecture. When a researcher lacks hard evidence, conjecture is his greatest tool. Some conjecture better than others. Some conclusions are more conclusive than others. There is one paramount factor, one compelling reason, why I have pursued this investigation. It comes from my understanding of the life of Moses. For those of you who may have forgotten your

Bible history, or never learned it: Moses was born in Egypt, put in a basket in the bulrushes, and claimed by a queen. The queen took Moses into her house as her own son, and hired Moses' true mother as the baby's nursemaid.

Moses, although an Israelite, was raised as an Egyptian and was supposed to gain the throne of the country. As it turned out, when Moses was older he saw an Israelite and an Egyptian fighting and came to the aid of the Israelite, killing the Egyptian. This was not only inappropriate in those days, but was a criminal offense as well. After all, Egyptians were superior to Israelites and killing an Egyptian was punishable by death. No questions asked.

Once Moses' criminal action was discovered, he fled out of Egypt, to someplace where he met a woman, Zipporah, whom he took as his bride and with whom he fathered a child. After his marriage, he tended his father-in-law Jethro's flocks at Mount Horeb, or Mount Sinai.

This is our first indication from the Bible as to where one should start to look for Mount Sinai. We should find Mount Sinai exactly, precisely, in the area of Jethro's home.

Fleeing for Your Life

There is another conclusion you can derive from this basic data to determine where Mount Sinai should and should not be. Remember, Moses killed someone and was fleeing for his life. Now, let me ask you this question. If you killed someone in your country, wherever you lived—whether it be Canada, Mexico, England, Germany, or Saudi Arabia—and the penalty was death, where would you go? Would you stay in your own country? Or would you flee to another country?

I think the answer is self-evident. Certainly you would flee to another country where there would be no army looking for you. A country where you would be protected by its laws. A country where the act that you performed in the other country would not catch up with you.

Doesn't it make sense to assume that is what Moses did?

Accordingly, I believe it would have been extremely foolish for him to stay in Egypt. He would have gotten as far away from Egypt as possible. He would not have hidden in the enemy's camp.

As I will show in a minute, the traditional Mount Sinai location is in land controlled by Egyptian forces at that time. Let me ask another question. As Moses was leading the children of Israel out of Egypt, wouldn't he do just that? Lead them *out* of Egypt and not lead them into land controlled by Egypt?

I think the answer to that is again self-evident. Yes, naturally, Moses would not have kept the Israelites in a land dominated by Egyptians. He would have gotten the Israelites as far away from Egypt, as far away from the armies of Egypt as humanly possible. Remember now, Moses was to wander for forty years—could he have done that in land controlled by Egypt?

So if I can show you that the traditional Mount Sinai was in land controlled and dominated by the Egyptians, wouldn't you then agree with me that it is not reasonable that the traditional site could be the correct one?

The only possible exception is if we consider that Moses was not very intelligent, or was extremely lucky, and decided to hide in the enemy's camp—decided, when his life was in jeopardy, that he could go to a mountain somewhere under the domination of the Egyptian armies. And then, when he was leading God's chosen children out of Egypt, he did not really lead them out of Egypt, as we were told, but simply led them into a different part of Egypt, then wandered for forty years amidst his antagonists. Not only does that not make good sense, it certainly is not congruent with how a leader of Moses' stature would function. Nor is it consistent with archaeological evidence.

A Controlling Point

The question becomes: was the area now considered Mount Sinai under Egyptian control during the time of Moses, or not?

If it was under the control of Egypt, I suspect you will agree with us that it is not a logical place to look, that the real mountain must be in some other place. So let's study that issue.

Not much is mentioned in the Bible of Moses' childhood. We are told that in his younger years he definitely took the side of the Egyptians and saw the Egyptians and not the Israelites as his brothers. It was not until later, after the incident in which he killed the Egyptian and, according to *Harper's Bible Dictionary*, "was forced to flee Egypt," that he sided with the Israelites. That squares quite well with what the Bible itself says. In fact, Exodus 2:15 says that when Pharaoh heard of Moses' killing of the Egyptian, "He sought to slay Moses. But Moses fled from Pharaoh's presence and took refuge in the *land of Midian*, where he sat down by a well" (emphasis added).

In the story of Moses' first visit to Mount Sinai, when he originally fled Egypt, we are given an important direction as to where Mount Sinai should be.

Exodus 3:1 says: "Now Moses kept the flock of Jethro, his father-in-law, the priest of Midian; and he led the flock to the back *or* west side of the wilderness, and came to Horeb or Sinai, the mountain of God."

In 2:19, when Moses' soon-to-be father-in-law asks his daughters why they came home so early that day, they replied: "An *Egyptian* delivered us from the shepherds."

In Exodus 3:7 we are told that God said: "I have surely seen the affliction of my people who are in *Egypt*, and have heard their cry" (emphasis added).

In 3:8 God continues, saying: "I have come down to deliver them *out of* the hand and power of the Egyptians" (emphasis added).

In 3:10 God said: "I will send you to Pharaoh, that you may bring forth my people, the Israelites, *out of* Egypt" (emphasis added).

Exodus 4:19 reads: "The Lord said to Moses *in Midian*, Go *back to Egypt*; for all the men who were seeking your life [for killing the Egyptian] are dead" (emphasis added).

It seems to me that whether you are Christian or Jew, Hindu

or Buddhist, Moslem or Scientologist, the message from the Bible is pretty clear. Moses left Egypt. Wherever he went, it was outside of Egypt. Therefore, Mount Sinai must be outside of Egypt. That certainly fits well with what a fleeing man would do.

Another view of the boundaries of Egypt can be gotten by reading *Smith's Bible Dictionary*. It states that Egypt "is a country occupying the northeastern angle of Africa." Certainly there is no argument over that. Smith continues, saying: "Its limits appear always to have been nearly the same." Also, as Smith points out, in Ezekiel 29:10 and 30:6: "The whole country is spoken of as extending from Migdol to Syene," which indicates the same limits to east and south as at present.

While the experts may disagree on many things, including the location of Mount Sinai, there seems to be little disagreement about who controlled the Sinai during Moses' years.

W. M. F. Petrie, writing in *Researchers in Sinai* (1906), says the Egyptians were in the Sinai area, the southern Sinai at that, and the proof was in many prehistoric Egyptian tombs. Turquoise was found that could only have come from one place—the Sinai. In fact, a petroglyph tells of over 730 people working in one group in the turquoise mines not far from the tourist version of God's mountain.

It is generally accepted that the Egyptians did not have much interest in the northern part of the Sinai Peninsula other than the trade routes connecting them with the rest of the world. From approximately 5500 to 1150 B.C., Egyptians worked in turquoise mines, as well as copper mines, in the area currently associated with Mount Sinai in the Sinai Peninsula.

Petrie claims that some 200 donkeys were used in the mining operations, with copper being smelted at Wadi Nasb. Proof of this is a tablet, found in the Sinai Peninsula, which has an inscription that was found to be by an Egyptian ruler who lived approximately 1887–1849 B.C.

Even now, one can find large quantities of copper smeltdowns at Wadi Nasb. Some of these reach a height of almost seven feet, and are anywhere from 200 to 400 feet long.

Here then is evidence that Egypt had control and domination

over the traditional Mount Sinai during Moses' time. One of the opponents of the traditional site, H. Palmer, writing in *Desert of the Exodus*, points out that this general area is in the region of the Egyptian royal mines. Palmer says the Israelites would not have moved in that direction for fear of the Egyptian army, which was camped in the area of the mines.

The grave of King Zaire contained turquoise mined from Wadi Maghara in the Sinai Peninsula. Such mining appears to have taken place around 5300 B.C., based on Petrie's documentation in *Researchers in Sinai*.

Petrie points out that another monument was unveiled from King Sanekht, approximately 4950 B.C. This monument carried writings indicating what took place in the quarries. All of these archaeological findings indicate that Egyptians were active in this part of the peninsula in the 5500–5000 B.C. period.

Rameses II and III both had activities in this area, something which has been ascertained by the discovery of mining operations, petroglyphs, and monuments. One small temple at Serabit el-Khadim contains a room that has almost twenty inches of ashes, most likely from burnt offerings. These offerings were probably offered to the mistress of turquoise.

This was no small operation taking place in Sinai. There were approximately twenty-five classes of quarry employees. Eleven ranks and titles were bestowed upon the local bureaucracy.

This area was hooked up with the Cairo area by oceangoing vessels, which put in at Abu Rudeis and an exchange of supplies and goods was made for copper and turquoise. We are also told by Petrie that "Egyptians established a magnificent temple here in the Sinai, because they discovered turquoise and copper at Serabit el-Khadim."

On the site of Wadi Nasb was discovered a tablet from the time of Amen-em-hat III, king of Egypt (1849–1801 B.C.). In this wadi, or ravine, for a length of 170 meters, a width of 100 meters, and depth of 3 meters, there are numerous heaps of copper dross. This dross is estimated as 1,000 tons of copper. There are also caves from which turquoise was mined. It is instructive to note there are no signs of copper mines in the whole region, so that the ancients must have brought the copper ores from the northwest of Jabal Musa, another mountain that, in the past, has been proposed as the real Mount Sinai.

Obviously, a lot was taking place in the Sinai Peninsula during Moses' time. In fact, it was infiltrated by Egyptians.

Petrie claims that there were no armies in the mines of the Serabit regions. But there is a strong conflict on this, as there are many contemporary relief drawings depicting wars or battles between the kings of Egypt and local inhabitants, most likely nomads.

Petrie says, however:

> If there is evidence that there is a militia at the time of Mer-ne-Ptah, then there must have been an army during the reign of the other kings, as well, for the following reasons:
>
> A. The Egyptian mines were royal property.
> B. They were the only copper mines of the Pharaohs throughout the land of Egypt, and the rulers acquired great wealth from them.
> C. These mines were in the desert outside the territorial border of Egypt, which passed to the east of the delta. Thus, it was essential that the output of the mines be defended, both from theft by the miners and the Nomadic desert tribes who moved along the transportation routes. We can only deduce from the inscriptions found in the mines that the mine workers were foreign slaves who would require constant guarding to prevent their escape.

In Werner Keller's fascinating book *The Bible As History*, we also find that "500 years before Abraham's day there was a flourishing import-export trade on the Canaanite coast. Shipping golden spices from Nubia, copper, and turquoise *from the mines at Sinai,* linen, ivory, and silver from Taurus" (emphasis added).

Perhaps Keller can best bring to light what Petrie truly found at Serabit el-Khadim. He said it was complete with "representations of cultic acts and pictures of sacrifices on the walls of the temple, indicating that this was the center of worship of the [Egyptian] Goddess Hathor. An also endless confusion of half-choked galleries in the neighboring wadis bore witness to the search for copper and turquoise. The mark of the workman's tools were unmistakable. Tumbled-down settlements, which house the workers, lie in the immediate neighborhood."

Petrie's greatest find was some script, known as the Sinai Inscriptions, which apparently goes as far back as the middle of the second millennium B.C. Petrie took this text and inscriptions with him back to England and waited for someone to crack the code to see what it actually said.

Keller tells us: "Paleographers from all countries pounced upon these awkward looking scratched type characters. No one was able to make any sense of them. It was not until ten years later that Sir Allan Gardiner, the brilliant and tireless translator of Egyptian text, lifted the veil."

Harper's Bible Dictionary says: "Sinai had contacts with neighboring regions, but the earliest significant evidence of such connection dates to 2650 B.C. At this early date the Egyptians began mining Sinai's turquoise—an enterprise that led to later Egyptian activities in the peninsula. Most famous are the turquoise and copper mines at modern Serabit el-Khadim in west-central Sinai.

"There was work throughout most of the 2d millennium," the *Dictionary* continues. It seems the evidence is rather conclusive. There was Egyptian activity taking place in this area where the current Mount Sinai is believed to be.

With this knowledge we can ask some interesting questions that I think give important answers. And the answers are that the true Mount Sinai cannot be in the Sinai Peninsula.

First, let's not forget that once Moses returned to Mount Sinai with the Israelites, he then wandered in that vicinity for forty years. And clearly the Sinai Peninsula was where the Egyptians had the leverage, the upper hand. If Moses were to have wandered in this area for forty years, it seems almost certain he would have encountered the Egyptian influence and his battles would have been with the Egyptians, not the Amalekites and others. Not once in the story of Exodus are we told that Moses ran into Egyptians in his forty-year wandering.

It may make sense to hide in the enemy's camp if your party consists of one or two, but Moses' party, based on Biblical testimony, consisted of 600,000 people. Perhaps a third of these were able-bodied men, the rest being women, the elderly, and children. Is this the type of group you would want to take to hide in the enemy's camp, especially if the camp, the Sinai Peninsula, was an extension of the country you were fleeing? Again the answer is, I think not. It would have been difficult for Moses to spend some forty years in the Sinai Peninsula in an area where the Egyptians were known to be active miners and to have an army standing by to protect the treasures plucked from the earth.

That, though, is really part two of the Exodus story. Part one is when Moses fled Egypt, fearing for his life, and went to Mount Horeb the first time. We can ask similar questions about that. Wherever he fled, we believe, he would have been outside of Egypt—certainly out of sight of the Egyptian armies and miners.

Perhaps this point is made the most tellingly by Jethro in Exodus 18:10, who says: "Blessed be the Lord, who has delivered you out of the hand of the Egyptians and out of the hand of Pharaoh, who has delivered the people [Israel] from under the hand of the Egyptians."

This reiteration of the Israelites' being out from under Egyptian domain simply does not—cannot—fit with the undeniable fact that a mere forty miles from St. Catherine's (the tourist version of Mount Sinai) there were Egyptian mines and a standing army.

And remember, Moses spent forty years with Jethro and his family, tending sheep in the area of Mount Sinai, wherever that mountain happens to be. Does it seem logical that Moses, as a simple sheepherder, would have been able to survive in an area of such strong Egyptian influence, as the Sinai Peninsula was even that long ago?

It is easy to twist logic around. I trust I am not doing that in this argument. Twisting logic is what gets people into so much trouble. But reanalyzed and simply stated, the logical thought sequence is that Moses' life was in danger, so he fled—fled his country, and naturally would also have fled any place where the Egyptian army was or had influence. Therefore, he could not have gone to the Sinai Peninsula. To do so would have placed his life at risk.

Accordingly, we reject the true Mount Sinai as being in the southern Sinai Peninsula. It is simply impossible for us to envision that Moses and his tribe of 600,000, or 60,000 (if you take some people's lesser number) could have survived for forty years in an area so dominated and controlled by the Egyptian army and mining community.

Here Moses would not have been able to wander forty years. He would have been hustled back to Goshen and executed. No David Copperfield or Harry Houdini could have hidden that many people for that long a time in an area that has limits to its size, especially based on grazing considerations. Wherever that many people went, they would have been noticed, and such notice would have been reported to the Egyptian army, who would have swooped down on them.

Don't think for one minute, though, that this is reason enough to refute the traditional Mount Sinai. There are plenty of other reasons the traditional site simply can't be the real one.

I'd like to start with the casual, and then work into arcane bits of archaeology and Biblical history, which also indicate the site must be found somewhere outside the Sinai Peninsula.

There are two ways to determine that the traditional site is simply not suitable for the encampment of Moses.

You can go and look for yourself as Bob and I did, or you can study the literature on the area. It will also, I am certain, convince you that the Monastery of St. Catherine and the traditional site are far afield from where Moses would have gone. If you visit the area you will be impressed, as we were, with its beauty. It certainly is not the beauty of the Swiss Alps or Glacier National Park. It is a desert beauty, one of vast sunsets and sunrises, hot days, and relatively cool nights. Above all, what will strike you about this land is how desolate it is. Desolation, of course, is a relative thing. A city in Oklahoma is desolate compared to New York City.

No Room at the Mountain

The base of the traditional Mount Sinai is so desolate it could not support a population of more than a few thousand people, certainly no more than 3,000.

One authority, Dr. Roy Knuteson, has stated: "The camping area, for instance, is not at the foot of this mountain, and cannot even be seen from the plain . . . measurements of the proposed camping area indicate there would have been less than one square foot of ground per person."

This makes for an interesting point: how could Moses have camped at the base of Mount Sinai for eleven months with (according to Biblical testimony) 600,000 people, or even 60,000 or 6,000 people?

The facts are simple. He could not. There is simply no camping place at the bottom of St. Catherine's monastery for an encampment of such magnitude.

All we are talking about here is physical structure. Is there acreage for this type of an encampment? The answer is no, there is no acreage for this type of an encampment. But let's, for the sake of argument, assume there was. Assume they all had quadruple bunk beds and in some sardinelike fashion squeezed themselves around any mountain in the Sinai Peninsula. The question then arises, could they have lived there?

Anyone who answers that in the affirmative is giving a spurious reply.

There is not enough vegetation in the immediate area of St. Catherine's monastery, the traditional Mount Sinai, to sustain a thousand people for eleven months, let alone the numbers the Biblical or archaeological scholars claim comprised the Exodus group. Our photographs, herein, reflect some of the desolation of this area. But most important, if you look closely you will see there is no vegetation. Unless Moses' people and livestock learned to eat rocks, they would have gone hungry.

Additionally, another important element is missing: water. There is barely enough water for the few tourists who struggle up St. Catherine's, let alone an encampment of 600,000 people.

According to Professor Manashe Har-El's writings in *The Sinai Journeys,* we can look at how many people are currently living in the Sinai area to get a sense of what this land will support. He says: "Epstein reported a census taken of Bedouins in the Negev in 1931 showed a population of 47,981 Bedouins, that is 4.3 persons per square kilometer, as against a density of 0.4 persons per square kilometer in Sinai." He then quotes a table from Ammar which gives the census for the Bedouin people in the Sinai area: "In 1882 there were a total of 217 Bedouins living in southern Sinai. By 1937 there were 2,449."

Professor and author J. L. Burckhardt estimated the population of most of the Sinai Peninsula at the beginning of the nineteenth century to be only some 4,000.

Even today, this is one of the most sparsely populated areas in the world. Yet we have pipelines, plumbing, electricity, the ability to dig wells and build roads, all of which weren't possible during Moses' time. And still the land cannot support much life. This is as true today as it was in the time of Moses.

This is just not the type of country that supports many people. That is the reason, and the sole reason, so few Bedouins are found in the area, even now.

Can you comprehend an area that currently has less than 4,000 people living in it at one time sustaining 600,000?

Of course not!

Equally important to consider is the tremendous amount of damage, physical damage, that would have been done to the fauna and flora of the area, let alone the damage to the land itself. A tribe of 600,000 people or even 60,000 people would have left its impression in perpetuity in the Sinai area. No archaeologist has found any indications of such a visitation. Reread that sentence one more time. It is staggering.

Perhaps the greatest Biblical scholar of all time, Josephus, makes it clear and concise in his writings: "The area around the true Mount Sinai was, by comparison, verdant and rich with pastureland." Certainly that is not the case of the traditional site. The rugged, craggy mountains of this area are almost exclusively comprised of stone. Good old-fashioned dirt and earth are precious and hard to find. In the wettest of years, the rocks would not sustain the Exodus.

A few years ago, the governor of the Sinai Peninsula claimed there were only fifty acres of agricultural land in the entire region! This certainly would not be enough to camp on for the masses expected from the Exodus, let alone their animals.

Remember, the Israelites spent a good deal of time at the mountain. If you believe Deuteronomy 1:6, you know for sure some time was spent at the mountain. We are told: "The Lord our God said to us in Horeb [Mount Sinai], You have dwelt long enough on this mountain." Most scholars say eleven months.

Again, if one believes the Bible, we have two good reference points here. First of all, there must be an area to graze sheep. Moses kept a large flock for Jethro. How large a flock we are not told, but a traditional flock of sheep can run anywhere from 50 to 500.

I don't think there is anyone who will contest that it is impossible to graze a flock of sheep at the base of the supposed Mount Sinai.

Then again, we get another reference, which is that the flock of sheep Moses tended was on the back, or west, side of the wilderness.

If you look at a map of the impostor mountain, you will find that it is not on the back or west side of a wilderness. If one were to envision a wilderness in the area, it would be to the north of the supposed mountain, and the Bible would have told us that Moses led his flock to the south of the wilderness—

certainly not to the west of the wilderness. There is no wilderness to the west of the traditional site.

Later on we will show that our mountain of Jabal al Lawz is to the west of a wilderness area. And there is ample room for a flock to be tended at the base of this mountain. For now, let's content ourselves with a more Biblical description of the pastureland that should be apparent at the true mountain.

Exodus 18 tells us that on his return to Mount Sinai, Moses met his father-in-law, Jethro, who told him how to administer his tribes. Jethro came to where Moses was "encamped," again a reference to a camp at the base of a mountain. Keep in mind, there is no room at the St. Catherine's site.

Boundary Markers

Exodus 19:12 also provides some interesting information, which we will return to later on in the description of what we believe to be the true Mount Sinai. This verse tells us that Moses was told by God: "You shall set bounds for the people round about, saying, Take heed that you go not up into the mountain or touch the border of it. Whoever touches the mountain shall surely be put to death."

There should be some pillars or markers around the base of the mountain indicating these boundaries. Additionally, there should be room for these markers to be set around the mountain. The traditional site does not afford the possibility of such markers—and more critically, none have been found there.

Cassuto claims: "The Torah emphasizes, again and again, that this barrier can by no means be demolished."

In Numbers 11:21 we are given a specific account when Moses said to God: "The people among whom I am are 600,000 footmen; and you have said, I will give them meat that they may eat a whole month."

Clearly there was a large group of people here and these people would have had a large amount of livestock, and no remains have been found at the traditional site, which only makes sense, since there never was any room to pasture them there in the first place.

Whether you should choose to go there yourself or look at our photographs or other people's photographs, one thing stands out. The mountain is barren, it is beyond desolate, it is void of what would be needed to support life for any substantial amount of people.

It is these bare facts that most strongly make the case that this is the wrong location.

There is another topographical problem with this being the true Mount Sinai. It is that Horeb actually means dry, dryness, or dry ground. At first thought, one would think this an adequate description of the traditional site. But one runs into two problems here as well.

The first is that while the traditional site appears to be dry, it in fact gets wet at certain times of the year. It gets wet during the winter time. It doesn't get wet from rain, but from snow. The top of the mountain gets snowed upon. In fact, when we were there in January 1988, there was snow atop the mountain. Some authorities have concluded that Mount Horeb (dryness) must be a dry mountain all year round, that it could be rained upon, but it should not have water other than a stream coming out someplace. Frankly, I think this is a moot point. It is arguable whether or not dry implies no snow.

Another thing is for certain: a mountain cap of snow would be an extremely difficult mountain for Moses to climb. Remember he made several trips up and down the mountain, most likely in winter or early spring.

Given the fact that Moses would have been approximately eighty years of age when he climbed the mountain (without the luxury of tour buses and steps carved into the side of the mountain by Christian monks), a physical inspection of the traditional site tells us this is a difficult mountain to climb, especially wearing sandals and carrying tablets of stone.

Now of course anything is possible in Biblical stories. And Moses, being a man of God, is entitled to perform a few supernatural tricks of his own. Yet there are other mountains that fit all of the descriptions and are not nearly as difficult to climb as this one.

When you put forward the two points set forth in this chapter, you find it exceedingly difficult to consider the traditional Mount Sinai as anything but an impostor.

It stretches one's credulity to think that God would have taken Moses and the Israelites to a mountain where there was no room for them to camp, no vegetation for them to eat, no water for them or their flocks, and then requested a Herculean effort from Moses to climb up and down the mountain—all this taking place in an area known to be inhabited by the enemy, in an area where the enemy kept and maintained regular armies, which would include scouts and a communication system to alert them to potential raiders of their treasures. It is not enough to say that given this information the traditional Mount Sinai would be questionable. It is more than questionable; it is simply beyond comprehension that this site could be the Biblical mountain of God.

Bob Cornuke, who spent time at the traditional site, has strong convictions about what it would sustain even in the twentieth century. Here are his thoughts:

> We traveled to Mount Sinai from Goshen in the traditionally accepted route. The first problem I had in believing that could be the mountain was the terrain leading to it. It was very difficult to pass—very thin wadis, sheer cliff areas, and a maze. It is hard to believe that many people could really migrate easily to that area, and also sustain life here.
>
> The vegetation was so skimpy. I did not see any sheep near the mountain, nor any shepherds with their flocks for many miles. I saw wild camels in the area, but there were no nomads moving sheep around—at all.
>
> There was an area at the base of the mountain for a small camp but no vegetation or water. No old streambeds can be seen in the area. It snowed the night before, so there was a dribble of water or melted snow forming a trickle of water. There was evidence that there could be some water

at St. Catherine's, but very, very minimal. I could not see how they could survive in that terrain. It was totally different in Arabia where we found grass and foliage enough to support flocks of sheep, with a large water source.

I do not see how this site could be the real one. The top of the mountain did not have any dark rocks indicating there was fire or flame there.

At the top of the mountain, you will find a little monastery or chapel for worship. Stairs had been cut into the mountain. Without them, it would have been a most difficult climb for all but experienced rock climbers.

There were a lot of people climbing the mountain for recreation. There were snow flurries there in the winter and it took about an hour and forty-five minutes to climb the 3,000 feet. I looked very carefully; there were no caves, when Biblical testimony mandates caves to be on the correct mountain.

There was no vegetation on the mountain, no trees, no shrubs. I cannot see how anyone, let alone a million people, could survive there. I have an aerial photograph from the top of the mountain showing there are mountain peaks all around and very little area where anything could grow or sustain life. I just can't see how anything could survive there, or close by.

It appears absolutely impossible to get people and livestock into that area. There are wadis and very difficult sand drifts. It would have taken forever to wind in through there. I don't know what Moses would have been doing there, tending his flocks. The vegetation has not changed over the years.

Looking from the top at a 360-degree view, there were just mountains all around. There were no camps, tents, or Bedouins. I did see a few Bedouins walking with camels, twenty to thirty miles away. The only people living there were the monks in the monastery.

Here is a fair question: if the traditional site is questionable—and so many years have passed since the Exodus—how can we ever know where the real mountain is? There is an answer . . .

3.
How Do I Know? The Bible Tells Me So!

As I documented in the previous chapter, without using the Bible as the only source, there is ample evidence to establish which mountain is, or is not, the real Mount Sinai.

The evidence presented in the previous chapter is not subject to debate. It simply is the way things are. No one would think that someone fleeing from an enemy would go to where the enemy lives, no one can suggest that 600,000 people could camp at the base of St. Catherine's monastery for eleven to twelve months. These things speak for themselves.

When it comes to the Bible, though, it is a whole different ball game. The Bible can be interpreted in a great many ways. Whether you choose the interpretation of Charles Manson, Pope John I, Terry Cole Whittaker, Pat Robinson, Jerry Falwell, or your local minister, people do read the Bible and come away with totally different interpretations.

What follows in this chapter, we hope, will have as little of our interpretation in it as possible, and more of what the Bible actually says. How do we get around this conundrum? By assuming that the Bible is written factually, correct as it is.

I am certain that you are aware that there are two major ways of approaching the Bible. One is that it is allegorical and that things that are said there should not be taken literally. The other is that they must be taken literally.

It seems that on the surface of things it does not make sense to write the Bible in an allegorical fashion; if it is to be the Word of God, it should be that—the Word—and consistent with the facts as set forth in that Book. This philosophy should be particularly true of the historical chapters, like Exodus, which were written to leave a record of events.

That is the approach we will take. At all times we will try to take what the Bible says and apply its absolute statements, without bias or interpretation, to establish where the true Mount Sinai is.

It is a bit confusing, regardless of which interpretation one uses, because it is authored by numerous people over different time periods. Nonetheless, we became convinced that the overwhelming Biblical evidence illustrated that Mount Sinai could be found only outside the Sinai Peninsula. And accordingly it was one of our motivating factors in our dangerous adventures of 1988.

Turn to the Bible

Let's first turn to the Bible for a physical description of what should be at the true Mount Sinai. This is a description, not an allegory.

In Deuteronomy 9:21 it is told that when the people were worshiping the golden calf at the true Mount Sinai, Moses said: "I took your sin, the calf which you had made, and burned it with fire and crushed it, grinding it very small, until it was as fine as dust; and I cast the dust of it into the brook that came down out of the mountain."

Well, here is one thing that needs to be at the one and only Mount Sinai. A brook coming out of the mountain. Is there such a brook coming out of the traditional site? No. It simply isn't there. Nor is there any evidence that a brook was there at any time.

I have already quoted from Exodus 3:1. Let's look again at that passage. As you might recall we were told: "Moses kept the flock of Jethro, his father-in-law, the priest of Midian; and he led the flock to the back or west side of the wilderness, and came to Horeb or Sinai, the mountain of God."

Clearly then, to fit this description, there must be to the east of Mount Sinai a large wilderness area. As discussed earlier, not only was there no place for Moses and his father-in-law to tend flocks at the base of the traditional Mount Sinai, there was no place to the east of the mountain for a flock.

To the east of Mount Sinai one finds only mountains all the way to the Red Sea. There is no room for flocks of sheep. Look at a topographical map to see our point.

We are also told Moses was wandering in the wilderness, which would suggest a plain or desert area, not a mountain area. Obviously, wandering with 600,000 people in the mountains makes no sense. Instead of a tribe of Israelites, it would have to have been a herd of billy goats. We are also given a geographical reference here, as we are told that Jethro was the priest of Midian.

This should cause serious researchers to quickly turn to maps to find out where Midian is or was. If you happen to have a Bible with maps, turn to the back pages to see what it says about Midian. If not, consult the map we have provided for the location of Midian.

Midian derives its name from one of Abraham's sons. We are told in Genesis that Abraham took "another wife" and she bore him Zimran, Jokshan, Medan, Midian, as well as Ishbak and Shuah.

Where Is Midian?

The Midianites have always been counted as "people of the East" and *Harper's Bible Dictionary* defines the word as "a general designation for the nomadic inhabitants of the Syrian and Arabian desert, Land of Midian. That part of Northwestern Arabia bordering the Gulf of Aqaba's eastern shore." There appears to be no dispute among Biblical scholars that the land of Midian is to the east of the Gulf of Aqaba.

There is no mention in any work we have been able to uncover that the land of Midian was ever reputed to be in the Sinai Peninsula. It was always to the east of the Sinai Peninsula across the Gulf of Aqaba, where the Kingdom of Saudi Arabia is now found.

This fits quite nicely with Exodus 18:3, where we were told that Moses fathered two sons with his wife, Zipporah: "And her two sons, of whom the name of one was Gershom [meaning expulsion, or a stranger there], for Moses said, I have been an alien in a strange land." (This said after he first fled from Egypt.)

Here we were given an explicit statement from Moses. Moses claimed to have been in a strange land, and felt strongly enough about it that he so named one of his sons. (Incidentally, for trivia buffs, Moses' other son was named Eliezer, which means "God is help.")

Exodus 18:1 reiterates the description of Jethro as "the priest of Midian."

The point to be made here is that, clearly, the traditional site in the Sinai Peninsula is not in Midian, nor is it even close to Midian. It is not in a place where shepherding was common, then or now. And since it was under the control of the Egyptians, it would seem strange (if that's where Moses went) that he would name his son Gershom, implying that he, Moses, had been an alien in a strange land. Moses was no stranger to Egypt, it was his birthplace!

This question of whether or not Mount Sinai is in Arabia is a telling point, and is one upon which the thrust of our argument will fall, because we have found a mountain in Arabia which fits almost all of the qualifiers.

The Bible has more to say about the location of Mount Sinai and Arabia. In Galatians 4:25 (KJV), Paul's letter says: "For this

Agar is mount Sinai in *Arabia*, and answereth to Jerusalem which now is, and is in bondage with her children" (emphasis added). In fact, directly north of Jabal al Lawz sits Jerusalem on almost a perfect north–south axis—in bondage together—the mountain and the city.

This attests to where the true Mount Sinai is. It is in relationship or in correspondence to Jerusalem and, in fact, is in bondage with Jerusalem.

It's clear from Paul's writing that Mount Sinai is not in Egypt; it is in Arabia. At this point it becomes perplexing. Why have Biblical scholars and archaeologists sought to establish Mount Sinai in Egypt, as opposed to Arabia? There is a reason. They have not been good mathematicians, as we show later. They have used poor math, believe it or not, only because they could not count higher than three. For now, though, connect a line due north of Jabal al Lawz and you'll bisect Jerusalem! Amazing, isn't it?

In Exodus 16:6 we are told: "So Moses and Aaron said to all Israel, At evening you shall know that the Lord has brought you *out from* the land of Egypt" (emphasis added)—another clear reference that they could not be in the land or confines of Egypt, but had to be some other place, "out of," not in, Egypt.

The mathematics of the Exodus are extremely important. We will touch on those later, at which point we will come back to Exodus 19:1, where we are told: "In the third month after the Israelites left the land of Egypt, the same day they came into the wilderness of Sinai." In other words, the mountain is about a three-month travel from Goshen.

Again the description is simple: Mount Sinai is not in Egypt. But notice that it wasn't until three months after they left Egypt that they came to the land of Sinai.

Let's get back to Midian now, as Moses was trying to do. Exodus 2:15 says: "When Pharaoh heard of it, he sought to slay Moses. But Moses fled from Pharaoh's presence and took refuge in the land of Midian where he sat down by a well." This refers to Moses' first flight out of Egypt after he had killed an Egyptian.

Not only is it surprising, but somewhat alarming, that Biblical scholars have not paid attention to the references to Midian in Exodus.

For example, take chapter 2 of that book starting in verse 16, where we are told that the seven daughters of the priest of Midian went to draw water to fill the troughs for their father's livestock. Apparently shepherds in the area came and drove the daughters away, but Moses, who was there, came to the daughters' rescue to help them water their flock.

A compelling question is asked in verse 18. Jethro, the priest of Midian, asks, "How is it that you have come so soon today?" The girls' answer is equally revealing. Remember now, the traditional view is that they were in Egypt, not Midian. Now think of that as you consider their answer.

Verse 19 tells us: "They said, An Egyptian delivered us from the shepherds; also he drew water for us and watered the flock."

Doesn't that strike you strangely? That in Egypt the daughters would have referred to Moses as an Egyptian? That's like saying in California if someone from California helps you that you were helped by a Californian. But if someone from Florida stopped to help fix your flat it would be logical to say he was a Floridian.

It appears from this testimony that Midian has no relationship with Egypt. If Midian was in the land of Egypt, there would not be reference to an Egyptian. While this might be circumstantial, certainly we have the cartographical evidence that virtually all authorities see Midian as being on the east side of the Gulf of Aqaba and not on the Sinai Peninsula.

Later on we will make a case for the Red Sea being named for the Edomites, and if that's the case, then the east branch, which is known as the Red Sea, would be the only true Red Sea, while the west branch would simply be the Gulf of Suez and not known as the Red Sea. I point this out here because the land of Edom is closely tied with the land of Midian on the maps you should now be looking at.

Verse 16 says: "Now the priest of Midian had seven daughters," again a concrete reference to where Moses went—Midian, not Egypt. So Exodus 4:19 says: "The Lord said to Moses in Midian, *Go back to* Egypt for all the men who were seeking your life are dead" (emphasis added).

In Numbers 10:29 we are told that when Moses was out of Egypt and at Mount Sinai, wherever it is: "Moses said to Hobab, son of Raguel the Midianite, Moses' father-in-law, We are journeying to the place of which the Lord said, I will give it to you; come with us and we will do you good; for the Lord has promised good concerning Israel." In 10:30: "Hobab said to him, I will not go, I will depart to my own land and to my family." Hobab, a Midianite by Biblical testimony, is telling Moses here that he has no desire to leave his homeland of Midian.

Again we are given the implication that Midian is somewhere in the area of Mount Sinai. You may wish to read all of Numbers 25 and 26, which contain clear references to Midian and Midianites. The basic point of these chapters is that the Midianites led Israel into idolatry. God then commanded Moses to seek revenge by destroying them.

One can turn to other sources to substantiate our view that Midian cannot be in the Sinai Peninsula.

One of the best reference sources of all Bible studies is *Smith's Bible Dictionary*. He says: "The Midianites as true Arabs . . . like Arabs, who are predominantly a nomadic people, they seemed to have partially settled in a land of Moab . . . dwelling principally in the desert north of the Peninsula of Arabia. Southward they extended along the eastern shore of the Gulf of Aqaba."

Even as far back as the ninth edition of the *Encyclopaedia Britannica*, we are told that the Midianites "probably always lived east of the Gulf of Aqaba." This pinpoints one, and only one, country: Saudi Arabia. How can anyone construe this to mean Egypt?

A Scholar Is Surprised

In the preparation of this book, I had an interesting experience. Bob and I had the pleasure of visiting one of the world's leading Biblical Egyptian scholars. In the living room of his home we carefully laid out our thesis—where the crossing took place, and why Mount Sinai should be found in Saudi Arabia. Almost instantly he said, "You are absolutely wrong! Mount Sinai must be found in the land of Midian. Therefore, to find Mount Sinai in Saudi Arabia is an impossibility."

I was perplexed. Had I done something wrong in my research? Had I really bungled this thing? I didn't know what to think. I carefully read from my notes a couple of the references cited above, and the retired professor said, "Here, I'll show you."

With that, he went to his library to bring out a geographical reference. He opened it to Egypt and looked to find Midian and was flabbergasted—in fact, I would say he was shocked—to find that Midian is not in Egypt, but is in Saudi Arabia!

Fearful as I am that I will bore you with the number of times that the Bible specifically mentions Mount Sinai as being in Arabia, let us move on to what other physical characteristics one should find at Mount Sinai.

According to the First Book of Kings, 19:8, we learn: Elijah "arose, and ate and drank, and went in the strength of that food forty days and nights to Horeb, the Mount of God [Mount Sinai]." Next verse 9: "There he came to a cave and lodged in it; and behold, the word of the Lord came . . . to him."

Make no mistake about it, First Kings is referring to a cave. In that same chapter, verse 13, we are told: "When Elijah heard the voice, he wrapped his face in his mantle and went out and stood in the entrance of the cave."

An Important Cave

The existence of the cave is of particular importance. While it is possible that the size of the Israelite encampment could have been exaggerated over the years, or the type of mountain could have been misdescribed, and a great number of other errors could have taken place in the Biblical recording, it is clear there needs to be a cave on the real Mount Sinai.

Bob Cornuke saw no cave—and he looked very hard to find one—on the traditional Sinai Peninsula site.

Another specific formation should be at Mount Sinai, in this case at the base, if one believes Exodus 24:4. Here the Scriptures say: "Moses wrote all the words of the Lord. He rose up early in the morning and built an altar at the foot of the mountain; and twelve pillars representing Israel's twelve tribes." Wherever the real Mount Sinai is, there should be twelve pillars somewhere near the base, and an altar.

Exodus 20:24 tells us God requested: "An altar of earth you shall make to Me, and sacrifice on it your burnt offerings." And 20:25 continues: "And if you make Me an altar of stone, you shall not build it of hewn stone."

I seriously doubt that an altar of earth would have survived all these years, but an altar of stone? Yes, I believe that in an arid desert such as exists at the traditional site, or the one that we feel is indeed the real Mount Sinai, a pile of stones (whether it be built a year ago, 1,000 years ago, or 4,000 years ago) has a pretty good chance of surviving. Thus, one should be able to locate some type of altar at the base of the true Mount Sinai.

Unfortunately for the Egyptian Tourist Society, none exists at the base of their attraction.

The traditional Mount Sinai site has been prodded, poked, dug, X-rayed, photographed from space, excavated, and checked with metal detectors and pendulums in search of the pillars and the altars. To date, no one has found anything remotely resembling altars or pillars of that time period. They are not there. Yet they should be. It is difficult to comprehend that a mountain as important as this one would be defaced or have all of the altars whisked away by someone. That doesn't make sense.

No Evidence in Egypt

Our good friend, Dr. Roy Knuteson, senior pastor of Waukesha Bible Church in Waukesha, Wisconsin, writing in *Confident Living* (Dec. 1988), tells about the famous Israeli archaeologist,

Itzhag Deit-Arieh, who spent over fifteen years in geological research in the Sinai Peninsula, specifically in the traditional Mount Sinai location. He came out of his wilderness wanderings to state: "There is absolutely no evidence where the Biblical reference or sojourn took place in that desert land."

Other man-made constructions should also be around the mountain.

Let's not forget that Moses' brother Aaron also had an altar constructed, where he worshiped the golden calf. Thus, in addition to the altar we are told that Moses built and the twelve pillars, one should find an altar site where the golden calf was worshiped.

Alas and alack, that also has not been found to exist anywhere near the traditional site. In the First Book of Kings, 19:8, we are also told that the true Mount Sinai was a forty-day journey from Mount Carmel for Elijah when he sought solace at the mountain of God.

Here one could argue, and argue well, that the Sinai Peninsula mountain is approximately a forty-day hike from Mount Carmel. However, it is only fair to point out that there are many, many mountains an approximate forty-day hike from Mount Carmel.

A good deal of evidence relating to the Exodus and Mount Sinai can also be gleaned from Exodus 32:27, where we are told that, in punishment for worshiping the golden calf, God directed Moses to tell his people to go out, "slay every man, his brother, and every man his companion, and every man his neighbor."

Exodus 32:28: "And the sons of Levi did according to the word of Moses; and there fell of the people that day about 3000 men."

The interesting point to make here is that we have a body count of how many Israelities were killed: 3,000 *men*, not families. This would suggest that the estimate some people have of Moses' tribe being 6,000 is far too low. This would also suggest the interpretation (whether it is 6,000, 60,000, or 600,000) must be at least 60,000. Because, otherwise, to kill 3,000 men would have left Moses with nothing but women and children.

One should be able to find the graves and some remains of 3,000 people killed at the base of Mount Sinai. Again, while the traditional tourist trap has been kicked and dug, and who knows what else, no bones of this time period have been uncovered—no pottery, no fragments, no armament, nothing. The area is as devoid of remnants of the Exodus trip as it is of vegetation and habitation.

One should also be able to find some type of burning activity having taken place at the top of the true Mount Sinai, at least if one puts much stock in the Book of Exodus. We are told in Exodus 24:17: "And the glory of the Lord appeared to the Israelites like devouring fire on the top of the mountain."

Exodus 19:18, 20 tells us: "Mount Sinai was wrapped in smoke, for the Lord descended upon it in fire; its smoke ascended like that of a furnace, and the whole mountain quaked greatly . . . the Lord came down upon Mount Sinai, to the top of the mountain. . . ."

This, if our Biblical research is correct, is the one and only place, according to the Bible, where God physically descended to planet Earth. No wonder the mountain would be burned, scorched, and who knows what else.

Some authorities claim this passage indicates a volcanic mountain; we disagree: the mountain was touched by God, hence the smoke, fire, and quake, not the other way around.

A similar account is given in Deuteronomy 5:4, where we are told: "The Lord spoke with you [the Israelites], face to face at the mountain out of the midst of the fire."

Again in Deuteronomy, in 5:22–23, we are told: "These words the Lord spoke to all your assembly at the mountain out of the midst of the fire, the cloud, and the thick darkness, with a loud voice . . . and when you heard the voice out of the midst of the darkness while the mountain was burning with fire. . . ."

I need to confess there is a slight problem here. Let's assume the Bible is categorically correct in what it states, that there was a large fire, a burn, on top of the real Mount Sinai. The real question is, Would there still be evidence after all these years, almost 3,500 years, of the remains of a fire on top of a mountain? Frankly, I think it is debatable. But my partner in this effort, Bob Cornuke, thinks our mountain site *is* scorched and will present that evidence later on.

Bob thinks that wherever Mount Sinai is, it should show a scorched top and evidence of burning. I'm not certain any mountain that high, 6,000 to 8,000 feet, whipped with wind and the elements over the millennia would still show signs of burning. Its absence would not necessarily mandate that a mountain could not really be the true Mount Sinai, but its presence would be a powerful persuasion that one had located the real mountain.

For the record, the Egyptian version of Mount Horeb does not indicate any burning at its peak or on any other part of it.

When one looks at all the physical descriptions the Bible has given of the appearance of Mount Sinai, trying to be as friendly as we can to the current widely accepted view, we can find only one instance where the mountain fits—it's approximately forty days from Mount Carmel.

With that exception, we cannot find any physical descriptions of the mountain from the Bible that match with the traditional mountain.

You may choose not to accept our view of what one should find at the mountain, but we think it will be widely accepted by Biblical scholars. Parallel research has been done by most other authors. Even the *Encyclopaedia Britannica* has said: "If the record of Exodus is strictly historical, we must seek a locality where 600,000 fighting men, or some two million souls in all, could encamp or remain for some time, finding pasture and drink for their cattle, and where there was a mountain (with wilderness at its foot) rising so sharply that its base could be fenced in, while yet it was easily ascended and someone could be seen by a great multitude below. In the valley there must have been a flowing stream."

The *Britannica* continues, saying: "The peninsula Sinai does not furnish any locality where so great a host could meet under the conditions specified. And accordingly, many investigators give up the statistics of the numbers of Hebrews and seek a place to fulfill the other conditions."

But Bob and I were not content with giving up the word of the Bible because the terrain did not fit. That would imply that the terrain is more important than the word. So, we concentrated on . . .

4.
Mount Sinai—
What Should Be
There

What Should Be There?

The task confronting someone trying to establish the location of the real Mount Sinai is tantamount to solving a mystery without the benefit of any living eyewitnesses. All we have to deal with is Biblical description, circumstantial evidence, and deductive reasoning.

Fortunately, the Bible gives adequate description of what should and should not be at Mount Sinai. Some of these things can be logically deduced, while other bits of information about the mountain are specifically stated.

We will work going from generalities to specifics in this chapter to give indication of the things we feel should be at the true Mount Sinai, wherever it might be. The most obvious, and certainly the one most scholars have touched on so far, is that there must be plenty of land for an encampment at the base of the mountain. And the Bible consistently refers to the Exodus taking Moses and his people outside of Egypt.

No place in the Bible is this more evident than in Numbers. In 11:5, the people tell Moses: "We remember the fish we ate freely *in Egypt*" (emphasis added). Obviously the Exodus people couldn't think they were still in Egypt and make that type of comment.

God himself, in Numbers 11:20, tells Moses that he will feed his people until they are satiated, until food comes "out at your nostrils, and is disgusting to you: because you have rejected and despised the Lord Who is among you, and have wept before Him, saying, Why did we come *out of* Egypt?" (emphasis added).

Exodus 16:6 reads: "So Moses and Aaron said to all Israel, At evening you shall know that the Lord has *brought you out from* the land of Egypt" (emphasis added).

We have provided numerous other examples of the Bible's reference of Mount Sinai being outside of Egypt, which is where we think one must look. I suspect there are over 150 usages of the phrase "out of Egypt" in both testaments of the Bible.

In Numbers 11:21 we are told: "Moses said, the people among whom I am, are six hundred thousand footmen [besides all the women and children] . . ." Depending on how one reads this, the footmen may or may not include women or children.

Enough Time, Enough People

There is another figure, though, that agrees with this. Let's take the Biblical time period that the Israelites were in Egypt (430 years—Exodus 12:40) and assume for the sake of mathematics that at the start of the 430-year period they had 100 people. This coincides rather nicely with a reference in Numbers to there being approximately 70, and those people increased at the rate of 2 percent a year. If so, at the end of 430 years, a 2-percent rate of growth would produce a total population of approximately 550,000 people.

Of course, if the rate of growth were slightly higher, let's say

4 percent instead of 2 percent, this figure would have been more than doubled.

The Distance Involved

A close study of Exodus, as well as Numbers, shows that there is some distance involved in the Exodus route. We referred to this earlier, but I want to highlight it one more time. Even prior to getting to the crossing site, time and distance are both referred to in the Bible.

This is clearly evident in Exodus 13:17–18, where we are told: "When Pharaoh let the people go, God led them not by the way of land of the Philistines, although that was nearer; for God said, Lest the people change their purpose when they see war, and *return to Egypt.* But God led the people around by way of the wilderness toward the Red Sea: and the Israelites went up marshaled [in ranks] *out of the* land of Egypt" (emphasis added).

Here we are given an indication that the Red Sea crossing site, wherever it is, is some distance away because God led the people "around by way of the wilderness." Obviously, it was not a straight journey to the Red Sea, wherever it was.

Verses 20–22 continue, saying: "They journeyed from Succoth and encamped in Etham, on the edge of the wilderness. The Lord went before them by day in a pillar of cloud to lead them along the way, and by night in a pillar of fire to give them light, that they might travel by day and by night. The pillar of cloud by day and the pillar of fire by night did not depart from before the people."

Again, from this passage, we think it reasonable to infer that this trip took some time. How many days and nights, unfortunately, we are not specifically told, but we are certainly given the impression that this was a journey of some distance, as the pillar and cloud were there "by day and by night." Therefore, it seems logical to conclude that wherever the crossing site is, it is a good number of days outside of Goshen.

In 14:2–3, we are given a description of the region of the crossing site, which is relevant to establishing Mount Sinai. We are told that God said to Moses: "Tell the Israelites to turn back and encamp before Pihahiroth, between Migdol and the [Red] Sea, before Baalzephon. You shall encamp opposite it by the sea. For Pharaoh will say of the Israelites, They are entangled in the land; the wilderness has shut them in."

Perhaps the greatest Biblical scholar of all time, Josephus Flavius, also recognized the importance of the necessity for a physical feature that would prevent the Israelites from moving farther. He describes it as follows:

> Now when the Egyptians had overtaken the Hebrews, they preferred to fight them, and by their multitude they drove them into a narrow place. . . . They also seized on the passages by which they imagined the Hebrews might flee, shutting them up between inaccessible precipices and the sea; for there was [on one side] a [ridge of] mountains that terminated at the sea, which were impassable by reason of their roughness, and obstructed their flight; wherefore they there pressed upon the Hebrews with their army where the [ridges of] the mountains were closed with the sea, which army they placed at the chops of the mountains, that so they might deprive them of any passage into the plain . . . while they were encompassed with mountains, and sea and their enemies, and discerned no way of flying from them.

The implication here is that there is something physical in the landscape itself that does not allow the Israelites to travel in any direction other than across the sea. They are, based on this testimony, essentially fenced in.

Only at the Straits of Tiran

Notice that this does not fit any of the proposed crossing sites that have been offered before. The only site this can possibly fit is at the Straits of Tiran. By our own observation, we saw that if the Israelites had traveled down to the tip of the Sinai Peninsula and turned slightly north at the base they would immediately run into mountain ranges that plunge into the ocean. At that point, the Israelites would be unable to continue up on the west side of the Red Sea. They would be hemmed in by the mountains and could not have gone back the way they came because the Egyptian army would be there. The Israelites would not have been able to "change their purpose when they see war" and return to Egypt.

At this particular point, and only this point, based on our physical studies of both branches of the Red Sea, is this Biblical criterion met. We are given more information of this nature in Exodus 14:10–12. There we are told: "When Pharaoh drew near, the Israelites looked up, and behold, the Egyptians were marching after them; and the Israelites were exceedingly frightened and cried out to the Lord.

"And they said to Moses, Is it because there are no graves in Egypt that you have taken us away to die in the wilderness? Why have you treated us this way and brought us *out of* Egypt?

"Did we not tell you *in Egypt,* Let us alone, let us serve the Egyptians? For it would have been better for us to serve the Egyptians than to die in the wilderness" (emphases added).

Two telling points come from these passages. First of all, the Israelites obviously are not in Egypt. There is continual reference to being outside of Egypt throughout Exodus and it is repeated here. The Israelites make it clear in four instances in these few verses that they are not in Egypt at the time the Egyptian army catches up with them prior to the crossing.

Also, it is apparent that the Israelites have no place to flee to. They are literally hemmed in. On one side there must be something—we are not certain what from the Biblical description—but something that does not permit them to proceed any farther in the direction they have been going. And second, the Egyptian army is behind them. In front of them they see an ocean which, at this point, they could not see a way to cross.

On Dry Land

There is another passage in this same chapter of Exodus that has received little or no attention from Biblical scholars but that we think is noteworthy. It is verse 22, where we are told: "And the Israelites went into the midst of the sea on dry ground, the waters being a wall to them on their right hand and on their left."

What is interesting to us about this is that it states rather clearly that at the crossing site one will not find mud or a sand bottom. One will find dry ground, footing that would make it possible to move horses and chariots over easily. An interesting thing about the Straits of Tiran crossing site is that there one finds, even to this day, a large land bridge. This land bridge currently, if it was without water, would give the appearance of being dry. You could drive a vehicle across it, with some trouble because of the coral growth, but it would be dry and stable ground. It would not be sandy nor would it be muddy.

Verse 29 of the same chapter reiterates, saying: "But the Israelites walked on dry ground in the midst of the sea, the waters being a wall to them on their right hand and on their left."

Obviously the waters were deep at this crossing site. They could not be shallow waters. If the water were shallow, let's say five or six feet, it would not have had the devastating impact we are told was caused by the reuniting of the waters.

Verse 28 says: "The waters returned and covered the chariots, the horsemen, and all the host of Pharaoh that pursued them; not even one of them remained."

Just imagine: "not even one of them remained." Obviously when the wall of waters came crashing down on the Egyptian army, it was of some magnitude. We're not talking here about water that was three or four feet deep, not even five or six feet deep, it must have been a huge amount of water that crashed onto the army to ensure that they all died—that not one of them lived.

This certainly does not sound like what would take place at one of the suggested crossing sites, the Lake of Reeds, or the Reed Sea, which is a comparatively shallow body of water. And since no artifacts have been found at this site, there is even more compelling evidence to think this body of water cannot be the true crossing site.

Chapter 15 gives further credence to this belief when we are told in verse 4: "Pharaoh's chariots and his host has He cast into the sea; his chosen captains also are sunk in the Red Sea."

Verse 5 continues: "The floods cover them; they sank in the depths like a stone."

The Exodus Timetable

A rough timetable is given in addition to these physical descriptions. In Exodus 16:1 we are told: "The congregation of Israel came to the wilderness of Sin, which is between Elim and Sinai, on the fifteenth day of the second month after they left the land of Egypt."

This means the Exodus was forty-five days old and they had not yet arrived at Mount Sinai, but had crossed the waters.

This is telling evidence of where Mount Sinai should be, and it simply does not coincide with the traditional St. Catherine's monastery site.

The St. Catherine's site is approximately 175 miles outside of the Goshen area. This means the tribe would have to have moved at a snail-like pace to reach the point that Exodus 16:1 refers to. This does not seem possible in light of the fact that the Israelites were being pursued, and, in fact, were fleeing for their lives.

To get to the site we believe to be the true Elim, it is about a 250-mile jaunt, which means they would have moved approximately six miles a day. This seems to fit better with the story of Exodus. While it would have been possible for the Israelites to travel as fast as eleven to fifteen miles a day, we think that once they crossed the Red Sea, the pace would have slowed considerably.

One thing for certain from this Exodus testimony is that Mount Sinai is not close to Egypt. It is not three or four days outside of Goshen, nor is the crossing site.

Certainly the Israelites did not stop once they crossed the

Red Sea. Obviously they would have recuperated and gathered their strength, as we have discussed. Numbers 33:3–49 lists the numerous campsites Moses founded for his people on the way to Mount Sinai.

The thrust of this commentary is that the traditional Mount Sinai location is not within Egypt and needs to be farther away than St. Catherine's. So this would, of course, apply to other sites that have been suggested, such as Mount Serbâl, or other Sinai Peninsula locations.

This does not rule out that another mountain in Saudi Arabia could be the true Mountain of Moses. It certainly does not conclusively prove that Jabal al Lawz is the true mountain. It is just suggestive, coincidental evidence indicating that our mountain is the right time and distance away to satisfy all the requirements of the Exodus.

What Moab Reveals

Let me briefly reiterate also, hopefully without being redundant, the importance of determining how many people were on the Exodus. If there were, say, only 500 people on the Exodus, they would need a much smaller area for their campsites than if there were 600,000 or more. (We are told in two places in the Bible, Numbers as well as Exodus, that Moses had with him some 600,000 men, not including women and children.)

The Book of Numbers is helpful in identifying how many Israelites were with Moses, because we are told in chapter 31 that the Israelites fought the Midianites in a great battle. At that battle Moses was directed by God to send 1,000 warriors from each of the tribes of Israel, which meant there would have been 12,000 men armed for war with the Midianites. This fierce battle took place on the plains of Moab, which is associated more with Saudi Arabia than with Egypt.

The plains are referred to in *Harper's Bible Dictionary* as being in the plateau east of the Dead Sea. This is generally accepted by other authorities, with Smith saying: "The Moabites first inhabited the rich highlands which were on the eastern side of the chasm of the Dead Sea."

Obviously, Moab is not in the Sinai Peninsula. This battle between the Israelites and Moabites provides us with a lot of information. We are told in Numbers 1 that the prey, not counting the booty which the men of war took, was 675,000 sheep, 72,000 cattle, 61,000 donkeys, and 32,000 persons in all.

For this type of battle to take place, even with a mere 12,000 warriors, the numbers indicate the Exodus tribe was no small thing to encounter. It must have been an incredible sight to see in the desert. Six hundred thousand people trudging their way across dry, uninhabited plains, followed by their goats, donkeys, and sheep, doing battle as they were willed to by Moses through direct intervention of God.

The Book of Numbers begins with a census taken by Moses "on the first day of the second month in the second year after they came *out of the land of Egypt*" (emphasis added). This census was of all male members of the Exodus gathering who were over twenty years of age.

In the first chapter of Numbers, the reader is given the name and listing of all the tribes. In verses 45–46 we are told: "So all those numbered of the Israelites, by their fathers' house, from twenty years old and upward, able to go to war in Israel, all who were numbered were 603,550."

Verse 49 points out that the tribe of Levites was not numbered in this census because God had directed Moses not to include them.

So again we have statistical data from the Bible itself which backs up the general idea of there being at least 600,000 people in the Exodus. Of course, there may have been almost twice this number of people, because this census limited itself to male members of the group twenty years of age and older.

Some Biblical scholars have pointed out that 600,000 may be a wrong translation of the Hebrew word *elip*, which the majority of the researchers have concluded means thousands. Some have said it may mean ten, some that it may mean one hundred.

The best evidence against *elip* as a lesser number is the tabulation in the first part of Numbers, where the tribes are broken down into smaller segments. And there is simply too much evidence in the Bible, given time and time again, to think the Exodus was smaller than 600,000 people, all requiring a campsite large enough to accommodate them.

The Pillars of Moses

Another specific physical requirement that should be at the real mountain of God is given to us in Exodus 24:4, where we are told: "Moses wrote all the words of the Lord. He rose up early in the morning and built an altar at the foot of the mountain; and twelve pillars, representing Israel's twelve tribes."

As Bob and I have described, on our second adventure into the fenced-off area at the base of Jabal al Lawz we came upon these pillars, and there is an altar at the foot of the mountain.

David Fasold is responsible for finding the pillars, which he did with electronic equipment. The pillars measure eighteen feet in diameter and are five feet apart. They are on a straight line that runs almost north and south from the guardhouse, which is at the northern part of the flat area in front of the mountain.

There is a wadi immediately in front of the pillars. The construction is not what one would think of as a typical pillar. At first glance, they appear almost to be tepee rings. The ring is comprised of three concentric stone circles. At this time they appear to be covered by dirt. It could be that dirt has washed over these pillars over the years, or the pillars are only three or four feet deep. That is a little hard to tell, especially at three in the morning, even with infrared scopes!

David had already discovered that there are twelve distinct pillars there. It would be unusual enough if there were twelve distinct rocks set up at the base of the mountain, let alone twelve circular columns this far out in the desert and at the base of the mountain. This seems to us to be indicative of Mount Sinai, and certainly in keeping with Exodus 24:4.

This is not the only physical evidence one should be able to find, based on a careful reading of Exodus.

Exodus 19:12 says: "And you shall set bounds for the people round about, saying, Take heed that you go not up into the mountain or touch the border of it. Whoever touches the mountain shall surely be put to death."

Verse 23 continues, saying: "And Moses said to the Lord, The people cannot come up to Mount Sinai: for You Yourself charged us, saying, Set bounds about the mountain, and sanctify it."

Verse 24 also refers to some type of boundaries around the mountain where God tells Moses: "Let not the priests and the people break through to come up to the Lord."

Shortly thereafter God gave Moses the Ten Commandments.

This indicates to us that one would expect to find some type of marking system—boundaries, stone markers, fence—some type of physical indication that would be easily seen by the Israelites who were told there was a line they should not cross, lest God "break forth against them" (Exodus 19:24).

In none of the discussions of the traditional Mount Sinai locations have we been able to find any reference to such boundary markers.

Boundary Markers at Jabal al Lawz?

Interestingly enough, we did find boundary markers, at least one could call them that, at Jabal al Lawz. These rock piles are approximately four feet high and about eight to ten feet in diameter. They scatter themselves like a semicrown about the base of the mountain and were measured to be three tenths of a mile apart. Standing on one of the boundary markers, you have a good line of sight on how these markers form a boundary that directs itself to both sides of the mountain. The boundary markers go essentially to the hills that form the mountains, thus giving a good demarcation line between the flat land, where people would camp, and the upstep leading to the mountain itself.

Of course, the reason for having boundary markers would be to keep the masses away from the mountain, which leads to the point we made earlier: wherever the true Mount Sinai is there must be room enough for a large camp area at its base.

This is not true of St. Catherine's, but *is* true at Jabal al Lawz. At the base of Jabal al Lawz there is a huge flat plain that fingers off up to several canyons in total. There is a valley itself that leads up to Jabal al Lawz from the Al Kan gas station. This is some twenty-five miles long and about one and a half miles wide. It is flat, and abundant with water.

This valley continues south of Jabal al Lawz, where it extends up into a large plain that is some fifteen miles long and seven miles across. Regardless of who looks at this area or how, one thing is for certain: Jabal al Lawz provides more than enough camping space for the Exodus.

Another point should be made at this time. We have been told in Exodus 32:28 of a battle site close to Mount Sinai where almost 3,000 people were killed. Allow me to set the stage.

While Moses was on the mountain talking with God and receiving the Ten Commandments, a large group of the people, led by Aaron, were doing their own celebrating. They had built a golden calf that they were worshiping and celebrating profanely.

On his way down from the mountain, Moses could hear the noises of jubilation; as he said in Exodus 32:18: "It is not the sound of shouting for victory, neither is it the sound of the cry of the defeated, but the sound of singing that I hear."

Moses went to see what the shouting was all about, only to find the golden calf, which he ground to powder, burned in fire, and scattered on the Israelites' drinking water.

Aaron was not man enough to take responsibility for creating the golden calf. He simply said that everyone who had gold took it off and gave it to him, and he threw it into the fire, "and there came out this calf" (32:24).

Moses was so angry that, after a quick consultation with God, he requested those who were on his side, and the Lord's side, to come with him: "Every man put his sword on his side, and go in and out from gate to gate throughout the camp, and slay every man and his brother, and every man and his companion, and every man and his neighbor" (32:27). Israelites slew Israelites.

Verse 28 specifically says: "And the sons of Levi did according to the word of Moses; and there fell of the people that day about 3000 men."

While this was not as large a battle as the battle of the Amalekites (as described in the following section), it does give a sense of the size of the tribe that Moses had at the base of the mountain.

The Amalekite Battlefield

The three events people associate most often with Mount Sinai are Moses receiving the Ten Commandments, the worshiping of the golden calf, and Moses striking the rock and having water come forth. Yet, as described in Exodus 17, an impressive battle took place in the area of Mount Horeb.

In verses 8–9: "Then came Amalek [descendants of Esau], and fought with Israel at Rephidim. And Moses said to Joshua, Choose us out men, and go out, fight with Amalek. Tomorrow I will stand on the top of the hill with the rod of God in my hand."

The ensuing battle must have been quite an event. Numerous scholars have attributed the Amalekites with warriorlike behavior. There are several references to this tribe as desert marauders, suggesting they were raiders of villages and agricultural areas.

Given that the Israelites comprised some 600,000 people, we can then reach an interesting conclusion about the size of the Amalekite group and how large the battlefield must have been.

If there were just 200 Amalekites versus 600,000 Israelites, the battle would not have lasted long. Even if there were 4,000 or 5,000 Amalekites versus the Israelites, they would have been overwhelmed rather quickly. We are told in Exodus 17:12: "Moses' hands were heavy and grew weary. So [the other men] took a stone, and put it under him, and he sat on it. Then Aaron and Hur held up his hands, one on one side and one on the other side; so his hands were steady until the going down of the sun."

There is the key point—until the going down of the sun. Obviously, this battle lasted some time. How long did it last? From sunup to sundown!

Envision, if you will, how many people must have been at this site for the battle to last ten to twelve hours, given that 600,000 Israelites were present.

Obviously, there must have been a great number of Amalekites as well, so there needs to be a gargantuan field for this battle to have taken place on.

This is another important feature that one should find close to Mount Sinai. This is particularly relevant, because Moses struck the rock from which water sprang out prior to the battle. So we know the battle site needs to be physically very close to the true Mount Sinai.

Moses went to a hill to view the battle of the Amalekites. So one should also be able to find some type of hill that would be out in the middle of a battle site area, or some promontory that would give Moses the ability to watch the battle as it ensued.

There is such a hill and there is a large flat terrain just south of Jabal al Lawz. There is no such physical or geographical configuration at any of the other Mount Sinai candidates.

The Cave of Elijah

One of the physical attributes that is sorely missing at all of the other potential Mount Sinais is the all-important cave of Elijah.

It's astonishing to think that scholars have continually accepted sites that do not possess a cave as potential Mount Sinai candidates.

The Bible makes it very clear in chapter 19 of First Kings, verses 8–9. We are told: "So he [Elijah] arose, and ate and drank, and went in the strength of that food forty days and nights to Horeb the mount of God. There he came to a cave and lodged in it; and, behold, the word of the Lord came to him, and He said to him, What are you doing here, Elijah?"

Verse 13 of the same chapter again refers to a cave. This is pretty simple. Elijah went to Mount Horeb (Mount Sinai), had a consultation with God, and he was inside a cave. This certainly couldn't have been Elijah stretching his imagination or some Biblical writer trying to color the story. The facts are quite simple. Elijah was inside a cave. For that matter, there is also reference to Moses' being inside a cave on Mount Sinai in Exodus.

The Altars of Mount Sinai

There are strong references in Exodus to at least two altars in the vicinity of Mount Sinai. The first that most people are familiar with is, of course, the altar where the golden calf was worshiped. This altar should be away from the mountain. And the altar rock site we have found at Jabal al Lawz is away from the mountain, outside of the boundary markers.

It is currently fenced in by the Kingdom of Saudi Arabia. However, our photographs clearly show the petroglyphs that have been painted upon these rocks. We unfortunately cannot read the minds of the kingdom to know why the rocks have been fenced off. It certainly implies on their part that they, too, think there is something of great archaeological significance here.

David Fasold received three very strong readings for gold on his metal detection equipment on his trip to the site. It was these gold readings that helped David find the twelve pillars. And it was also these readings that helped him find the pile of rocks where he found what he believes to be pictures of the golden calf being worshiped.

There is yet another site that David has revealed to me which should also show an abundance of gold once it is excavated. Hopefully, in combination with professional archaeologists, we can do some digging on this site and will not only produce remnants of the Exodus at the base of Jabal al Lawz, but also specific gold artifacts that would correctly date and tie everything together. I believe that the gold of Moses is one of the greatest treasures in the world today—and it's just waiting to be recovered.

In any event, we do know from studying Exodus 20:24–26 that God told Moses to have an altar of earth made for him where Moses would "sacrifice on it your burnt offerings and your peace offerings, your sheep and your oxen."

Verse 25 continues: "If you will make Me an altar of stone, you shall not build it of hewn stone; for if you lift up a tool upon it, you have polluted it."

And verse 26 says: "Neither shall you go up by steps to My altar, that your nakedness be not exposed upon it."

Another specific physical requirement that should be at the real Mount Sinai is some type of evidence (unless it has been totally destroyed) of an altar's having been in the area at the mountain base. It appears from these passages that the altar would be made of either uncut rock or dirt, and we would envision it to be of some size because of the type of sacrifices that would be made on it. The types of animals that God instructed Moses to sacrifice, as well as the number of people who would be presenting animals for sacrifice, imply we are not talking about a ten-by-ten-foot altar here. We are talking about something of some consequence.

The Altar We Found

The other suggested Mount Sinai locations do not have such altar sites, while at the base of Jabal al Lawz, Bob and I found on our midnight scramble what appears to be an altar of uncut stone. It is a six-sided affair that is essentially two long rectangles that meet in the middle, thereby giving a point (as you can see in our drawing of Mount Sinai). Each wing of this angular form is approximately sixty-five feet long and about thirty feet wide, with a dirt or rock mound that is spaced equidistant from

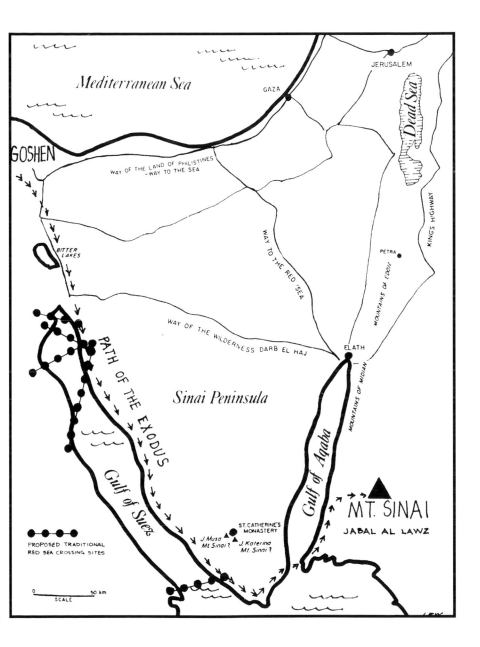

Mediterranean Sea

GOSHEN

JERUSALEM

GAZA

Dead Sea

WAY OF THE LAND OF PHILISTINES
- WAY TO THE SEA

BITTER
LAKES

WAY TO THE RED SEA

KING'S HIGHWAY

PETRA

MOUNTAINS OF EDOM

WAY OF THE WILDERNESS DARB EL HAJ

ELATH

PATH OF THE EXODUS

Sinai Peninsula

MOUNTAINS OF MIDIAN

Gulf of Suez

Gulf of Aqaba

ST. CATHERINE'S
MONASTERY

J. Musa
Mt. Sinai?

J. Katerina
Mt. Sinai?

MT. SINAI

JABAL AL LAWZ

PROPOSED TRADITIONAL
RED SEA CROSSING SITES

0   50 km
SCALE

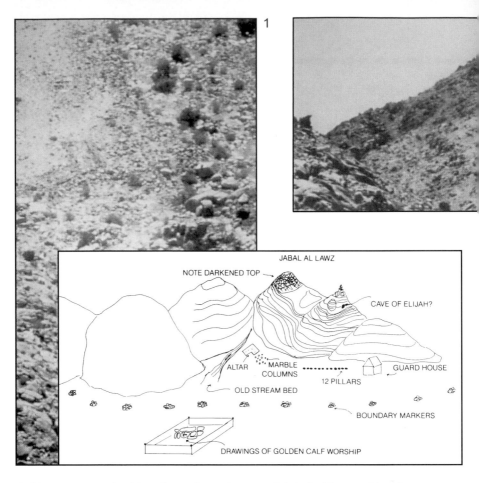

1

JABAL AL LAWZ

NOTE DARKENED TOP

CAVE OF ELIJAH?

ALTAR

MARBLE COLUMNS

12 PILLARS

GUARD HOUSE

OLD STREAM BED

BOUNDARY MARKERS

DRAWINGS OF GOLDEN CALF WORSHIP

1. Here, you are looking down from the top of Jabal al Lawz. Clearly, you can see the foundation of the temple we found at the bottom of this mountain. Around this temple, we found pillars, 21 inches in diameter, made of marble or quartz.

2. Jabal al Lawz. To be noted here is the darkened cap of this mountain. In the photograph it looks as though there might be a shadow over it, but the picture was taken on a cloudless day.

3. The construction of the rock pillars found at the base of Jabal al Lawz. "Moses wrote all the words of the Lord. He rose up early in the morning and built an altar at the foot of the mountain; and twelve pillars, representing Israel's twelve tribes" (Ex. 24:4).

4. Here is the cleft part of Jabal al Lawz. In dead center you can see the cave of Elijah. We've been told by local Bedouins that there are a good number of ancient inscriptions inside this cave.

5. This is the altar site where, we believe, the Golden Calf was most likely created, worshiped, then ground up and burned by Moses. Note the fence surrounding it that has been installed by the Minister of Antiquities.

6. Here you can see the guard house at the "caves of Moses," as well as the fence. This is a high-security area, although there are no military installations here, simply these caves or burial tombs in the hillsides of the mountain.

2

4

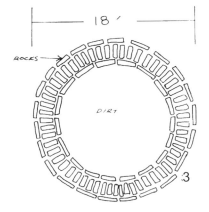

ROCKS

18'

DIRT

:3

5

6

7

8

7. The traditional St. Catherine's monastery site on the Sinai Peninsula of Egypt. This particular site was established by a psychic or seer, who advised Constantine that this was the mountain of Moses.

8. Red Sea land bridge in the middle of the Straits of Tiran, where we believe Moses led the children of Israel when the Sea parted.

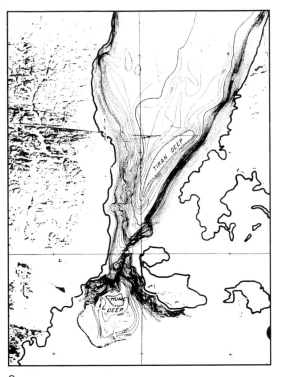

9. Bathometric map of the Straits of Tiran, where we suspect the Red Sea crossing took place. There is a spot known here as a Hume-Deep, which is the area of the ocean I believe the chariots, bodies, etc., from the disaster would have fallen. This area of the ocean definitely needs to be researched. As you can see from the topographical lines, there is a sandbar or reef that goes across this area. (Source: Defense Mapping Agency, National Oceanic and Atmospheric Administration)

10. Here you can see what the captain of this ship didn't see! The Jackson Reef caught this ship. It now sits at the Straits of Tiran, high and dry—clearly illustrating the reef that runs across from Egypt to Saudi Arabia.

11. Here, the author is shown standing on the land bridge that extends across the Straits of Tiran. The picture is taken looking back into Egypt.

9

10

11

12. This petroglyph was found at what we believe is the altar site. The archaeologists for the Kingdom of Saudi Arabia declared that this petroglyph, as well as those in photograph 14, are the Egyptian Hathor and Apis bulls.

13. This petroglyph was found close to the side of the mountain. It appears to show someone holding an animal (a calf?) above his head, and may well represent people worshipping the Golden Calf.

14. Is this the altar site of the Golden Calf? The two cattle-like petroglyphs were identified as Egyptian Hathor and Apis bulls by an archaeologist representing the Kingdom of Saudi Arabia. These petroglyphs are unique to this area; all others portray goats or camels.

15

16

15. If you look closely, you can see two dark spots approximately at the center of the mountain. This is one of the offshoots of Jabal al Lawz. Unfortunately, we were not able to get inside the caves.
16. Here Bob Cornuke is going to the cleft rocks, coming down from the pinnacle of Jabal al Lawz. Is this where Moses received the Ten Commandments?

17

18

17. This is the town of Al Bad, which seems to fit the Biblical description of an oasis of seventy palms and twelve springs—mentioned as one of Moses' stops following the Red Sea crossing. Nearby we located the caves that local tradition said were the caves of Moses, from which Moses and his followers went on to Mount Sinai.

18. This is another photograph taken by the roadside in Al Bad—the Springs of Elim, or the resting place of the springs of Seventy Palms. This is the first oasis coming north from the Straits of Tiran. It would have been approximately six days' travel for the Exodus group to reach this location.

19

20

19. Here you can see the caves, described by the local people in Al Bad as being the caves of Moses. Note what appear to be Egyptian fronts on these caves. We believe they were burial caves and most likely represent the area inhabited by Moses' father-in-law Jethro. There appears to be no research on or explanation of this site in any Arabic literature.

20. Amalekite battle site? The promontory in the exact middle of this photograph may well be where the Battle of the Amalekites took place. It is east and a little south of Jabal al Lawz, which fits well with the Scripture as to the battlefield. There does need to be a mound someplace where Moses would have sat, arms raised, to sustain the Israelite victory. We found no evidence suggesting this was the site; the site simply speaks for itself. It is close to Jabal al Lawz and has the correct physical features.

21

22

21. Scholars have long been perplexed that there are no sites at the traditional Mount Sinai for camping, or even water, for the Exodus tribes. As you can see from this picture (taken 4/~ mile from Jabal al Lawz), there's vegetation and an ample amount of room for campsites.

22. Here is another picture of the large camping sites available in the area of Jabal al Lawz. The rock mound in approximately the center of the photograph is the altar site where we found the petroglyphs that may well represent the worshipping place of the Golden Calf.

23

23. This is another view depicting the large, open space available at the bottom of Jabal al Lawz for the Exodus encampment.

24. The Springs of Marah? This hole was dug recently—notice the indentation 24
where a rope has pulled buckets of water out. We believe this is the area where,
as the Bible tells us, Moses turned the bitter water to drinkable water: there are old
alkaline lake beds here, and obviously plenty of water; it also fits the timetable of
Exodus 15:22—its distance from the Straits of Tiran (33 miles) would seem to match
with the three days it took to reach this spot in the Exodus journey.

the edges inside the form, which also makes an arrow or V-shaped appearance.

There are no steps going up to this altar site. The stones are uncut.

We have absolutely no idea what this formation is or what it is doing at the base of Jabal al Lawz. But some things we do know. It is not the foundation for a house because it does not allow enough space for any type of living quarters.

We do know that the apex or V of the structure points directly at Jabal al Lawz itself. We think that is significant but that may be just happenstance, and you, too, might feel that way.

The rocks have been carefully placed in formation. It appeared (of course, at three in the morning it's a little difficult to know exactly what you saw) that a good deal of time was spent in putting together the rocks of this site. Now, we have no absolute proof it is an altar. All that we know is that it does not fit the requirements for a normal physical structure. It is not only too narrow to be a house, but, of course, there is also the problem with the inside running piece. Ask yourself: what else could this be?

The most intriguing thing to me upon visiting this structure (which we will call an altar site for lack of better words) is that strewn next to it was a good number of what appeared to be marble pillars or columns. These are twenty-one and a half inches in diameter and are anywhere from twenty-four to thirty-two inches in height. Somebody, at some time, had another type of altar here. Whether it was for worship we do not know. The remnants of very nicely cut stones are there. We know, we saw them.

It is hypothetical, but we think someone came along after the Exodus and built another altar site here of cut stones. Apparently this later temple was torn down and most of the stones removed. The local Bedouins tell us the stones had been removed to Haql for a temple or monument erected by Solomon or Sulliman. This also needs to be investigated.

We were fortunate enough to come out with rock samples of

the polished material. Analysis of the rock samples indicated they may have been burned.

Most interesting, though, is that finding these polished columns at the base of Jabal al Lawz compares with finding polished columns of marble at the bottom of the Grand Canyon. In both instances the mere appearance of this type of foreign material is strange and should be subjected to further study. We can conjure all sorts of things that these temple stones may or may not mean. Further study is needed, not only of what appear to be the original temple stones from the uncut rock altar site at the base of the mountain, but also of these polished stones that imply a much more advanced civilization with the skill to deal with this material.

These stones are of material that is foreign to the area. Where the pillar stone came from, we don't know. We did not see any stone remotely similar to this in our travel throughout the Arabian desert. Someone had to bring the stone. It is extremely heavy and therefore difficult to carry great distances. These stones were carted here for a specific purpose. We would like to know what that purpose was, and suspect it would have to do with Jabal al Lawz's being a highly significant religious site. That seems to be the only logical conclusion to draw. Do you think that these polished stone pillars grew there, or found their way by happenstance?

There has never been a town at the base of Jabal al Lawz. Why would this type of material be at the base of the mountain? Oh, if only the stones could cry forth!

Given that the stone is polished and done in pillars, you might want to check through your own experience to come to some conclusion as to what these stones were used for. In our experience such columns are found only in two places: government buildings and places of worship. Certainly no government bureaucracy ever had an office at the base of Jabal al Lawz. That leads us inexorably to the other alternative, that this type of structure connotes religious worship of some sort taking place at the base of this mountain.

More Physical Evidence

Much has been made about Moses and the burning bush on Mount Sinai. The story is related in Exodus 3.

Perhaps the most telling point is not the burning bush. One wouldn't expect to still see a bush burning on the real Mount Sinai, wherever it is. Of course it would be great evidence, wouldn't it?

Chapter 3 begins: "Now Moses kept the flock of Jethro his father-in-law, the priest of Midian; and he led the flock to the back or west side of the wilderness, and came to Horeb or Sinai, the mountain of God."

If Moses were to lead Jethro's flocks to the back or west side of the traditional St. Catherine's site, he would find two things. First of all, there would be no place for the sheep, and second where would this place Jethro's residence?

However, at Jabal al Lawz it is an entirely different picture. If in fact Jethro's camp at Elim is the current town of Al Bad, it would be natural for Moses to lead a flock to the west side of Jabal al Lawz, which is to the east of Al Bad. This location also would place "the flock to the back or west side of the wilderness."

This unique geographical reference point (3:1) cannot apply to the traditional site, but can apply quite easily to our potential site.

We don't know, of course, if there should be evidence from some type of a fire near the summit as a result of the mountain's being scorched by God. This is referred to in Exodus 19:18, as well as Exodus 24:17 and Deuteronomy 5:4.

Don't take our word for it, take our pictures for it. The top of Jabal al Lawz is black and what caused that we frankly have no idea. But we do know, as you can see for yourself, the mountain is dark at the top. In fact, as you look at the photograph, you may think there is a cloud over the top of the mountain casting a shadow upon the mountain. But that is not the case. There wasn't a cloud in the sky the day these photographs were taken. That simply is the way the mountain appears; it has a darkened top. This is another element that the other mountains suggested as Mount Sinai do not possess.

One of the enjoyable things about studying the Bible is that it is jam-packed with reference points, if one will take the time to think about and cross-reference Biblical events. You are given a good deal of data about what took place, and where.

An example of this takes place in chapter 19 of First Kings, when we are told that Elijah went from the area of Mount Carmel "and went in the strength of that food forty days and nights to Horeb, the mount of God."

In other words, what we can deduce from this is that Mount Sinai is forty days' travel from Mount Carmel. The traditional St. Catherine's Mount Sinai location on the tip of the Egyptian peninsula is a long, tough forty-day travel from Mount Carmel. More likely, it is about a sixty-day walk from Mount Carmel. Whereas our location in Saudi Arabia would be quite doable in forty days.

Unfortunately the Bible doesn't tell us what shape Elijah was in—if he was a long-distance runner, a plodder, a mucker, or a sprinter. While the distances from Mount Carmel to Mount Sinai are not terribly conclusive, here they are more favorable for the Arabian site than they are of the traditional.

A final point needs to be made, and this is in regard to the battle with the Amalekites, as well as the killing within the Israelite tribes themselves (at least 3,000 people were killed according to Biblical data). One would expect that even a minor archaeological dig in the area of the true Mount Sinai would uncover a hoard of paraphernalia, ranging from burial sites, perhaps skeletons and armament, to indications of camping activity.

No such signs of the Exodus or similar encampments have been found at any of the suggested Mount Sinai sites on the Egyptian peninsula.

Unfortunately, we cannot yet confirm that any such artifacts exist at the base of Jabal al Lawz, but there is only one reason for that—it is not yet been dug.

The other suggested Mount Sinais have been researched and

sifted through, virtually with a fine-tooth comb. Our observations are that absolutely no archaeological activity has taken place on the site or surrounding areas of Jabal al Lawz, with the exception of what we have reported in this book.

We are told (Exodus 24:10) that on top of Mount Sinai: "They saw the God of Israel and under His feet it was like pavement of bright sapphire stone, like the very heavens in clearness."

This would suggest that there might be some type of glass or sapphire material on top of the real Mount Sinai. Wouldn't this be a great find for someone?

Such a discovery has not been made on any of the Mount Sinais that have been suggested through the years, and that includes Jabal al Lawz. We found no such material on top of the peak of Jabal al Lawz. There is a possibility that there might be this type of material on top of the false peak or the peak above what we had called Elijah's cave. Unfortunately, we did not visit that peak because it would have exposed us to the Bedouins encamped at the base of the mountain.

I think it is safe to say, however, that such material does not exist at the site. It certainly would be far from normal for sapphire or other glassy material to be discovered in this area of the desert.

We saw no such material on any of our climbs up the back side of Jabal al Lawz. And I seriously doubt one would find it on the other peaks. However, if one did, I'd bet my bottom dollar that we had, in fact, discovered the true Mount Sinai!

Well, there you have it. What should be and what should not be around and on top of the real mountain of God.

I hope you will be able to use this chapter as a reference to compare what we have discovered, a reference to filter out the story that we are presenting of our trips to Saudi Arabia, so you can better find . . .

5.
The Altar of the Golden Calf

If one were to look in the Bible for a man whose faith in God was tested the most, I think you would have to conclude it was Moses.

Throughout the Exodus, Moses was plagued with problems which it appears God, working through the Egyptians or the Israelites, put to him.

This is expressed well in Exodus chapters 32 through 35.

While Moses had gone to the top of Mount Sinai to have, if you will, a conference with God, the rest of the children of Israel gathered around his brother Aaron and in 32:1 began saying: "Make us a God to go ahead of us; for this is the way it is with Moses, the man who brought us up out of the land of Egypt, we do not know what has become of him."

The absence of Moses on top of Mount Sinai for almost forty days apparently caused the tribes to grow restless and impatient; without a leader, they turned to look for a new leader and Aaron was their choice. In 32:2 Aaron's reply was: "Take the gold rings from the ears of your wives, your sons, and daughters, and bring them to me."

We know the Israelites had much gold because they had taken many ornaments of gold and silver from the Egyptians just before the Exodus began. Aaron apparently melted the gold ornaments which were presented to him and made them into an idol, an idol in the shape of a calf, the golden calf which all students of the Bible know.

In the land which the Israelites had left, the Nile Valley, the cow was one of the sacred gods that the Israelites had seen Egyptians worship many times, and so it was a familiar image to them.

In 32:4 the people said to Aaron: "These are your gods, O Israel, which brought you up out of the land of Egypt." Aaron went one step further when he saw the people worshiping the cow, requesting that an altar be built for the golden image and said: "Tomorrow shall be a feast to the Lord" (32:5).

About this time Moses started coming down from the mountain with the Ten Commandments. On his way down with Joshua, Joshua said in 32:17: "There is a noise of war in the camp."

This gives us a good idea that the worship site of the golden calf should not be too far from Mount Sinai. It certainly should be within shouting distance and probably visible from the mountain as well, as Moses apparently saw the people dancing and singing about the golden idol.

The story gives us some helpful physical descriptions. There should be some evidence of an altar, it should not be too far from the mountain, and the calf or cow that was worshiped should appear Egyptian in nature.

Finally, we know that Moses burned and ground the golden calf and put the remnants in the drinking supply for the Israelites (32:20).

Interestingly enough, it appears from this description that the golden calf was not solid gold, since Moses "burned and ground" it; thus it seems the calf may have been a wooden object that was perhaps covered with gold. Perhaps it was gold-leafed, or gold was poured over it in some fashion, but the fact that the Bible specifically says it was burned and ground indicates that it was not a solid gold statue. Otherwise it could not have been burned, it could have been melted but not burned.

Local Legend

We would next like to turn your attention to the photographs we took that could well be described as a rock altar site. It is clearly visible from the peak of Jabal al Lawz.

Bedouins camped near Jabal al Lawz say there is an old story that a golden camel is buried near this mountain. Their specific word is "calf," but local Arabs assume that means the calf of a camel—it is an uncanny coincidence that local legend parallels the Biblical story.

Our estimate is that the altar site is approximately thirty feet high and the rock mounds comprise an area about eighty feet square. We were not able to get exact measurements because this area has also been fenced off by the kingdom. A large sign has been placed at the front saying: "THIS IS AN ARCHAEOLOGICAL SITE, DO NOT ENTER."

It is unfortunate that the government of Saudi Arabia has fenced off the site without providing any evidence of conducting further research regarding the site or what they think is the significance of the drawings on these rocks.

Frankly, one can argue that this altar site is too large to be man-made. There are several rocks that are sizable, yet there is an appearance, a man-made sense, to this mound of rocks because the rocks are just that, a mound, located in a middle of an otherwise flat area. Perhaps the mound of rocks is a natural formation and some type of altar was placed on top of this rock pile, which could be another possible way of using this site as an altar.

What is absolutely clear from the evidence of our photographs is that there are several drawings of a cow or bull at this altar site.

Intriguing to us is that the cow appears to be Egyptian in

nature. Note that the horns have the spiraling effect that one so often sees in the horn of the Apis, or Hathor, cows in Egyptian inscriptions. Compare our photographs with traditional Egyptian drawings and you'll see what we mean.

We feel this is a most unusual find to discover in the middle of Saudi Arabia, because the area is not one known for cattle, and the etchings in some instances are as big as six feet by four feet.

Expert Testimony

The kingdom's archaeologist, who represented the state at Fasold's trial for entering the area, testified: "These drawings are the Hathor and Apis bull from Egypt—I have never seen them in this country before."

While some people might contend that these are simple drawings of what historic inhabitants of the area were hunting for, we think that is a wrong notion, based on the fact that this is clearly not cattle country. This is sheep and goat country. There's not enough grass to sustain herds of cattle. There is also not enough surface water for such cattle. Cattle are not indigenous to the area in any way whatsoever.

None of the drawings show hunters shooting at or trying to kill the cow. In fact, some of our photographs show people appearing to be worshiping the cow, as they are holding the cow above their head. This strikes us as an extremely unusual picture for a hunter to draw of something he is hunting. Hunters like to draw pictures of killings, they like to depict themselves vanquishing their prey. None of these scenes can be found on the petroglyphs at Jabal al Lawz.

What may also be of significance is that we found two other locations that have similar etchings or paintings on rock. One of them on the back side of Jabal al Lawz also shows people apparently worshiping a cow as it is held above the arms of its bearer as though offering it to something or someone. None of these descriptions on the back of the mountain show the animal being killed. They do not reflect bows and arrows, spears, or other instruments of hunting. They simply are drawings of cattle and people holding cattle above their heads.

None of the drawings we found in the Jabal al Lawz locations depict the cattle being herded or being fenced in. We think that even to the biased observer this indicates some type of reverence or worship.

On the front side of the mountain, in addition to the rock altar site, we discovered another group of drawings the government has not yet fenced off.

This site, on the southern part of the mountain, is done in the same texture as the drawings on the altar site. Again, similar animals are depicted, although not as elaborate or ornate or as large as on the altar site. We also think that this is significant. Neither of the drawing sites found outside of the fenced-off area have work as accomplished as the drawings inside the fenced-off area on the altar site. Outside the altar we found crude stick drawings—inside the fenced-off area one sees major pieces of what may be Biblical art.

Both of the other locations have more than enough space for the elaborate large-size drawings of the altar site, yet they are not there. At the altar site one sees etchings of four to six feet—one may be over eight feet—while the etchings at the other sites are no bigger than ten to twelve inches.

One can only ask why. It certainly implies the altar site is of some significance. The other drawings depict the story of worship of a cow, but not nearly with the same graphic skill. They are lacking in the size and detail of those at the altar site, which causes us to think the rock protrusion is, in fact, an altar. Something was going on here other than people drawing caricatures of cattle, caricatures of an animal that is widely known not to exist in this part of Saudi Arabia.

Finally, an important point that needs to be stated about the altar site is that we know, unequivocally, from David Fasold's work that there is a substantial repository of gold close to this altar site—the gold of Moses brought out of Egypt?

Based on the readings David did with a molecular frequency generator, we are confident there is a substantial amount of gold at this site just waiting for archaeologists, or would-be archaeologists such as ourselves, to uncover.

This is most likely the gold the Israelites took out of Egypt and with them on the Exodus. We cannot tell from David's reading whether it is melted-down gold or precisely what shape it is in. It is our expectation that one would find the jewelry that worshipers of the golden calf deposited at this site when Moses came upon them.

Bob and I carefully scouted the area at the base of the mountain in our initial search for the altar site. We did not find, with two exceptions, any other drawings on any rocks on this or any other mountain in the area north of Tabuk.

An interesting book has been written by Jean Koenig, written in French and titled *Le Site de Al-Jaw Dans l'ancien Pays de Madin*. Koenig's thesis is also that Mount Sinai is in Saudi Arabia. He feels that it is another mountain. Unfortunately, our French is not good enough to understand all his assertions, but he has taken the liberty of showing a great number of drawings and petroglyphs from his proposed location.

In none of these drawings does one find cows, calves, or bulls. What one does find are drawings of camels, people riding camels, camel caravans, and all done in small stick figures. There are also a few drawings of what appear to be large birds, similar to an ostrich, and perhaps the ankh symbol from Egypt.

His suggested site is about 110 miles south of Jabal al Lawz. What interests us is that both sites are in the same general area, hence one would expect to see similar drawings in both areas. In fact, you do not. There is one, and only one, place where one finds the large bovine etchings done in the rock, and that is at the base of Jabal al Lawz.

This also seems significant to us. If it was a generally accepted practice for people to worship cattle in that area, or if there were cattle in that area at that time, what's found in one spot would appear in other spots throughout the desert. Nomadic tribes leave their mark every place they go—yet there are no similar drawings at any other spot in this entire region.

All this can only cause one to wonder, to question: what

are these manifestations doing at this particular site? If they existed here, in and of themselves, they might not be as significant as their existence in combination with other telltale facts suggesting we have uncovered more than a simple desert mountain.

In Summation

The basic facts are quite simple. We have what appears to be a rock altar with pictures of a cow worshiped long ago which Saudi archaeologists testified in court are of Egyptian origin. We also have drawings of people worshiping the cow, holding it over their heads. And we believe there to be a substantial quantity of gold at this site.

Given that gold is not endemic to this part of the desert, and neither are cattle, we think that one can only conclude that this altar is a significant archaeological find that needs a massive amount of professional and scholarly work done on it to determine its significance.

We conclude that it is most likely the altar which Aaron and the Israelites used to worship the golden calf.

To our way of thinking, everything that one would expect to find at the altar site of the golden calf exists on this pile of rocks in the midst of the desert. There may be other explanations but we have yet to run across anyone who can present a plausible thesis for what else could have taken place at this particular site.

Now, it may well be that any such worship site would have been destroyed in the ensuing years. We feel it is noteworthy, however, to point out that none of the other proposed Mount Sinais have claimed, or even discussed, the possibility of an altar site. It is necessary that one should be able to find an altar, or at least the facility for there to have been an altar site of some significance where the golden calf was worshiped.

In several of the sites there simply is no room available for such an altar site, and in none of the sites has anyone, to our knowledge, found anything approximating an altar site. Ye here in Saudi Arabia, we found something that not only approximated an altar site, but appears to be just that.

In this mystery without any living witnesses, the circumstantial evidence mounts high. Yet the battle goes on, only now it has become . . .

6.
A Scholarly
Battleground

There is yet another Biblical problem with the Egyptian version of Mount Horeb. It has to do with the battle that took place shortly before Moses arrived at the real Mount Sinai. The details are given in Exodus 17.

What this chapter tells us is that the Israelites had gone for three days without water and were getting thirsty. Accordingly, they started to complain to Moses. Moses then asked the Lord what to do and was told to strike a stone and water would come forth.

In verse 6, God says: "Behold, I will stand before you there on the rock at [Mount] Horeb; and you shall strike the rock and water shall come out of it."

Verses 8 and 9 say: "Then came Amalek, and fought with Israel at Rephidim. And Moses said to Joshua, Choose us out men, and go out, fight with Amalek. Tomorrow I will stand on top of the hill with the rod of God in my hand."

The following day a battle did ensue, which must have been substantial, considering that Moses had some 600,000 men in his troops. The battle lasted all day. Obviously, the Amalekite warriors must have numbered somewhere in that general area, maybe more, maybe less. But it certainly would not have been 20,000 against 600,000 for a battle that would last all day.

Even if you assume the lowest expectation of Biblical scholars of there being 60,000 people in Moses' traveling group, there would have been a comparable number of Amalekites (imagine 120,000 men battling hand to hand), which still means one needs to have a very large battlefield. Also in that battlefield, one needs to have a large hill or promontory for Moses to have witnessed the skirmish.

It is interesting to note that what apparently turned the tide for Moses that day was that when he lifted his arms the Israelites would win the battle. When he lowered his arms, the Israelites' fortunes would wane. To solve this problem, Aaron and Hur went to the top of the hill with Moses and held up his arms to make certain they would win the battle.

In fact, verse 12 tells us: "Moses' hands were heavy and grew weary. So [the other men] took a stone, and put it under him, and he sat on it. Then Aaron and Hur held up his hands, one on one side and one on the other side; so his hands were steady until the going down of the sun."

The question a serious detective needs to ask is, Who are the Amalekites, and where did they live? The answer to this would effectively pinpoint the real Mount Sinai, as we are told the battle of the Amalekites took place near the vicinity of the true mount. Thus, Mount Sinai could be designated, geographically, if one were to know where the Amalekites resided; for a battle this large it would have been the entire congregation of the Amalekites versus the Israelites.

In *Harper's Bible Dictionary* we are told that the Amalekites "inhabited territory assigned to Israel, Judah and the Jordan states." All these locations are "out of Egypt" far from the traditional site.

Smith's Bible Dictionary states that "Arabian historians represent them, the Amalekites, as originally dwelling on the shores of the Persian Gulf, once they were pressed westwards by the growth of the Assyrian Empire, and spread over a portion of Arabia."

Werner Keller's *The Bible As History* has three references to the Amalekites, all of which place them south of Jerusalem in the area of Saudi Arabia.

A second battle occurred with the Israelites, which may help give us more definition of territory. This is the battle referred to in Numbers 14:45, telling us the Canaanites and the Amalekites attacked Israel on the borders of Palestine. Neither of these battles is located in any proximity to Egypt, nor is either near the Egyptian version of Mount Sinai.

Some good and specific background of the Amalekites' homeland can be gleaned from *The Historical Geography of Arabia* (Vol. 2) by the Reverend Charles Forster. He says: "The classical boundaries of the Saracens geographically coincide with the Scriptural boundaries of Amalek, taking the Amalekites in the largest sense of the name, of the representatives of all the Edomite tribes throughout northern Arabia."

A specific location is given: "The positions of the Saracenic Tribes . . . is as follows . . . the line of country behind [or south of] Arabia Petraea, and Arabia Deserta, which forms the necks of Arabia Felix, is peopled by the tribe leaving Saracens. Their country was bounded on the north by the Stonian Desert, Arabia, and on the south, by the ancient Arabia Felix."

Forster continues: "The original seats of Amalek were in Sanaa, in the surrounding parts of Yemen; whence, the Amalekites emigrated, as invaders, first to the neighborhood of Mecca and Medina; and, finally, to the northern desert, and the frontiers of Syria and Palestine."

It almost gets a bit confusing to track which tribe was doing what, in that part of the world at that time, but one thing becomes clear: the Edomites and Amalekites were one and the same, or were part of a general culture in the area. Again, if you check any map (not just our maps, but any maps illustrating that time period), you will see that the land of the Edomites is not in Egypt, but in Arabia.

If you get confused with historians, I suggest you turn to the Bible, because there are numerous quotations that give you reference points to these people whom Moses fought.

For example, Numbers 13:29 says: "Amalek dwells in the land of the South, the Hittite, the Jebusite, and the Canaanite dwell by the sea, and along by the side of the Jordan."

The point made here is that there is a relationship among all of these locations. None of them are in Egypt. They are obviously related tribes, but all are far to the east of Egypt and particularly the traditional Mount Sinai (note there is no land south of St. Catherine's in the Sinai Peninsula for the Amalekites to "dwell in").

Numbers 14:25 tells us: "Now . . . the Amalekites and the Canaanites dwell in the valley [of Horeb, Mount Sinai]."

Several Biblical scholars have twisted the interpretation of where the Amalekites lived because they have assumed that Mount Sinai must be in Egypt. Thus, they have tried to push 600,000 Amalekite soldiers into Egypt while there is no reference to the Amalekites being in Egypt, especially in the traditional Mount Sinai area. Not only is there no Biblical reference to their being there, but no remnants or artifacts of the Amalekites have been found at the traditional site.

Indeed, no less a scholar than William Smith says in his description of Arabia: "Those from northern and western Arabia are other peoples which, from a geographical position and mode of life, are sometimes classed with the Arabs. These are the Amalek descendants of Esau."

It is intriguing when one reads the scholars to find they all give credit to the Amalekites as living in Arabia. They may not all agree on the exact valley or the precise site where they camped and dwelt; yet they all draw the same conclusion: the Amalekites were a group of Arabians. These same scholars then push them across the Red Sea, hoping to place them in Egypt at Mount Sinai, then later push them back into Arabia. We are not willing to do that.

The Amalekites Were Not in Egypt

We agree the Amalekites were in Arabia and dwelt close to Mount Sinai, thus indicating that the true Mount Sinai is also in

Arabia. There is no need to transport tribes across plains, valleys, mountains, and oceans, as their tribal grounds were in the vicinity of the authentic site.

The absence of any Amalekite evidence in the Egyptian Sinai Peninsula is one more stone around the neck of traditional Exodus archaeologists, carrying them down further in the quicksands of their argument that Sinai is in Egypt. If the Amalekites had lived in the Sinai area, we would have to conclude otherwise. But not one bit of Amalekite evidence has been found on the traditional site.

This is not just some small point; wherever Mount Sinai is to be found, one must also find evidence of the Amalekites. They go hand in glove with each other. Find the Amalekites and you should find Mount Sinai. Find Mount Sinai, and nearby you will find the evidence of dwellings of the Amalekites.

Since all authorities set Arabia as the home grounds of the Amalekites, that's where the real mountain will be found.

Before Moses got to the mountain of God, he first had to cross the Red Sea, in one of the Bible's most vivid, yet discounted, stories. The facts as given in the Book, we believe, show beyond a shadow of a doubt where and when the crossing took place. Yet other authors have missed this one key point. So it is now time for . . .

7.
Uncrossing the Red Sea Crossing

"It's About Time"

The major Biblical description historians and Biblical scholars have used to ascertain the true location of Mount Sinai has been the Red Sea crossing.

Most everyone in the world seems to know the story. Moses, while on the Exodus, was pursued by the Egyptian pharaoh, who thought he had Moses boxed in, because in front of Moses was the Red Sea, behind him Pharaoh's armies. Moses, however, with the help of God, parted the Red Sea, allowing his people to cross to the other side. When the armies entered the Red Sea in hot pursuit, they were not as fortunate. The sea, which had either receded or formed walls, collapsed back to its normal form, falling on and drowning the soldiers.

While that is the general story, when one turns minute attention to the Bible, there is a great deal more to learn from the Red Sea crossing. From close scrutiny of the crossing story, one can ascertain what type of body of water Moses crossed and about how many days' journey outside of Goshen the Red Sea crossing was, and get a good description of the terrain of the crossing site. That will be the purpose of this chapter.

It is our impression that for thousands of years scholars have made a critical and glaring error in their analysis of the Red Sea crossing. We will attack that first and then get into the details of the crossing site and its significance in locating the mountain of God.

A Question of Basic Math

The glaring error every scholar we have encountered has made is the assumption that Moses crossed the Red Sea three days after leaving Goshen.

In fact, though, that is not what the Bible says. Specifically in Exodus 3:18, Moses is quoted as asking the pharaoh: "The Lord, the God of the Hebrews, has met with us; and now let us go, we beseech you, three days' journey into the wilderness, that we may sacrifice to the Lord our God."

There is nothing in this verse about the Red Sea being three days away. Moses requested that he and his people be allowed to travel outside of the pharaoh's influence for three days, so that he might worship his God.

A growing number of scholars now feel the traditional three days' total journey is not correct. Their position is that while Moses initially asked for three days to go out into the desert to pray, once the Passover struck the Egyptians and Moses started to flee, all agreements were nullified, and Pharaoh became angered and decided to pursue Moses.

Most scholars agree that it would have taken Pharaoh a good deal of time to structure his militia and prepare them for the chase. Additionally, it seems only logical to conclude that Pharaoh would not be in a rush because he knew what he was chasing—not another army, but men, women, and children.

The question for the soldiers would not be *if* they would catch Moses and his clan, it would be only a question of *when*.

We feel, and we will discuss it shortly, that Pharaoh most

likely would have begun the organization of his troops about six days after Moses left. One could argue that Pharaoh would have immediately become angered at Moses and begun the pursuit right away, but there is no Biblical reference to that. And given the Plagues, it does not seem reasonable to expect such promptness on the ruler's part. Even at that, if the royal army began immediately, they would not have caught Moses before he had made it to any of the proposed Red Sea crossings.

Given the second scenario, though, Moses still would have about a three-day lead on Pharaoh before Pharaoh had thoroughly prepared his troops for the ultimate encounter. Thus, regardless of which view you choose to take on the starting point of the Exodus and Pharaoh's actions regarding Moses, you most likely get the same conclusion: Moses had a head start on Pharaoh.

The Importance of a Head Start

I should add, based on the study of Psalm 105, there is good reason to believe that Pharaoh would not have given chase a day or two, or even several days, following Moses' departure. After all, the Plague of Darkness had been cast upon Egypt; water was turned into blood; fish died; frogs were brought to existence throughout the kingdom; there were swarms of beetles and flies, and mosquitoes and lice. Instead of rain, Egypt was besieged with hail; lightning struck, appearing like flaming fire; locusts and grasshoppers came to destroy all vegetation; and finally, the killing of the Passover took place.

It is no wonder that Psalms 105:38 says: "Egypt was glad when they [Moses and his people] departed, for the fear of them fell upon the people." Accordingly, we think it is not good logic or a sign of good Biblical study to think that on the day Moses left, Pharaoh began his pursuit. Instead, clearly Moses had a head start of some consequence.

This view is further supported by the late professor of Bible Studies at Hebrew University of Jerusalem, Umberto Cassuto, who states in a commentary on the Book of Exodus: "The issue and implementation of the mobilization order took, of course, several days, and in the meantime the Israelites journeyed."

One might ask what type of group Moses had with him. There is not a lot of reference to this in the Bible, but Psalms 105:37 says: "There was not one feeble person among their tribes."

In Exodus 10:9, Moses tells his pharaoh: "We will go with our young and our old, with our sons and our daughters, with our flocks and our herds [all of us and all we have]; for we must hold a feast to the Lord."

In 10:28, Pharaoh says to Moses: "Get away from me! See that you never enter my presence again, for the day you see my face again, you shall die!" (How wrong he was on that!) When it came time for Pharaoh to let Moses go, he certainly had no qualms.

As you might recall, God told Moses to paint blood above the doors of all the Israelites so they would be protected during the sacrifice of the Passover. There was much death in the homes of the Egyptians during that night. Exodus 12:30 tells us: "Pharaoh rose up in the night, he, and all his servants and all the Egyptians; and there was a great cry in Egypt for there was not a house where there was not one dead."

Verses 31–33 continue: "He called for Moses and Aaron by night, and said, Rise up, get out from among my people, both you and the Israelites; and go, serve the Lord, as you said.

"Also take your flocks and your herds, as you have said, and be gone! And bless me also.

"The Egyptians were urgent with the people to depart, that they might send them out of the land in haste; for they said, We are all dead men."

As I've mentioned, there has been a considerable amount of debate on exactly how many people did travel on the Exodus. It appears that not all of them were Israelites, since a reference to a mixed multitude is made. So perhaps a census would not be exaggerated, but understated, because of these others.

A strict interpretation of the Bible shows that there were over

600,000 men, and in addition to that, women, children, and animals. This number comes from several places in the Bible, in particular, Numbers 1:46, and has caused many historians to conclude that something must be wrong with this figure, that it smacks of error, because it would be such an impossibly difficult group to move about.

Accordingly, several interpretations have developed. One is that the word "thousands" really refers to military contingents, which would mean there might be 600 of these military groups. Some authorities interpret the word "thousand" as tent group, which would mean, as an example, that there were some 600 tent groups, not 600,000 people on the Exodus, thus significantly reducing the number of people on the Exodus. Perhaps 60,000, not 600,000, was really meant.

Numbers 1:45–46, you remember, shows a total of 603,550 males over twenty years of age. This numbering is an accounting of men able to fight and available for combat. Numbers 26:51 gives a total of about 601,730 Israelites and members of the second generation of the Exodus.

There is one school of thought, though, that says that Numbers may be correct because it would show "the extent that God has graciously blessed Israel in multiplying the descendants to such large numbers." At least that is one of the theories in *Harper's Bible Commentary*. The *Commentary* continues, saying: "It is clear that the present form of the text intends for these figures to be taken as they stand, as in 'thousands' and not 'tent groups.' "

From what we can deduce so far, Moses asked to go outside of Egypt for three days' travel and was given permission. Egypt was in a state of shock, not only because of the killing of the Passover, but because God had struck Egypt time after time. As a final curse upon the nation of Egypt, as told in 12:35: "The Israelites did according to the word of Moses; and they [urgently] asked of the Egyptians jewels of silver and of gold, and clothing."

Verse 36 tells us: "The Lord gave the people favor in the sight

121

of the Egyptians, so that they gave them what they asked. And they stripped the Egyptians [of those things]."

So in addition to their flocks they carried a substantial amount of clothing and jewels, silver, and gold, but most of all the blessing of the Egyptians to leave.

In Exodus 13:18 we are given more evidence of the route of the Exodus. We are told here: "God led the people around by way of the wilderness toward the Red Sea. And the Israelites went up marshaled (in ranks) out of the land of Egypt."

Was there a reason to this? Yes, for God had said in verse 17: "Lest the people change their purpose when they see war, and return to Egypt." That is why there was not a direct route to Israel but a roundabout way through the wilderness and the Red Sea.

The Key Question

From this a natural question must arise: when would Pharaoh have learned that Moses was not going into the desert for three days to worship, but in fact was fleeing?

The answer is obvious. The soonest he would have learned of it was on the fourth day of the Exodus.

(Note here that if one follows the other alternative, that of Pharaoh's getting angry immediately after Moses had fled, we need to ask when he would have taken action. Does three to four days later seem sensible? We think so. Hence the following criteria play out the same.)

He could not have learned it any sooner. From this we can also judge that wherever the Red Sea crossing site is, it is at least four days outside of Goshen. It cannot be a shorter distance. In fact, as we will next see, it must be substantially farther in terms of travel days.

We will assume that Pharaoh's infiltrators were alert. They would have known on the fourth day that this was not simply a three-day jaunt into the desert. We believe that at the end of the fourth day they would have come to the conclusion that it was time to go back and tell Pharaoh that Moses was deceiving him. If Moses and his people are outside of Goshen four days, it's going to take approximately three to four days for the messengers to get back to the pharaoh.

Now, listen carefully to what next must take place. If the messengers take four days to get back, Pharaoh must gather his troops and get them ready to chase Moses. How long would that take? Given the fact that Egypt had been decimated by the power of the Lord, we assume a bare minimum of two days for the troops and soldiers of Egypt to be brought together and supplied; Exodus 14:5–7 tell us: "It was told the king of Egypt that the people fled, and the heart of Pharaoh and his servants was changed toward the people, and they said, What is this we have done? We have let Israel go from serving us!

"And he made ready his chariots, and took his army.

"And took 600 chosen chariots, and all the other chariots of Egypt with officers over all of them."

We surmise from these statements that there were some Egyptians traveling with Moses and the Israelites, or at best that Pharaoh was intelligent enough to have some of his troops (or spies, if you will) on what was to become the Exodus. And in some fashion, he learned that Moses was not just going into the desert for three days but was escaping the country. Remember, Moses did not ask for permission to leave Egypt, he asked only to go three days out to worship his God.

A Review

Let's review the math. Moses goes out of Goshen four days and he and his people are still moving. The pharaoh's messengers go back, up to a four-day trip, then add two days to prepare the army. So Moses may be ten days outside of Egypt before the pharaoh, all his army, and his 600 chariots begin the drive to their doom.

Obviously the pharaoh is going to move faster in pursuit than Moses can travel, because of the number and nature of Moses' people. After all, it is easier to move an army of 600 chariots and "all the other chariots of Egypt with officers over all of them" than it would have been for Moses with women and children, cats, dogs, goats, and cattle to make this Exodus.

Let's not forget, though, he was given some assistance—in this case speed—by his maker, as 14:20 tells us: "Coming between the host of Egypt and the host of Israel . . . was a cloud and darkness to the Egyptians, but it gave light by night to the Israelites; and the one host came not near the other all night."

In Exodus 13:21: "The Lord went before them by day in a pillar of cloud to lead them along the way, and by night in a pillar of fire to give them light, that they might travel by day and night."

And in 13:22 Exodus we are told: "The pillar of cloud by day and the pillar of fire by night did not depart before the people."

Thus, though Moses may have been slow, he was steady, with a guiding light so he could travel at night while the Egyptians could not.

Considering Moses was about ten days outside Pharaoh's reach before Pharaoh began his chase, the next question is how long would it take for Pharaoh to catch up with him.

Assuming for sake of argument that Moses travels at two-thirds the speed of the Egyptian army, it should take Pharaoh and his charioteers approximately six days from Goshen to catch up to the point where Moses was when Pharaoh began his pursuit. That would give Moses another six days to be traveling, putting him out a total of sixteen days. It would take Pharaoh approximately four more days to catch up to where Moses was at that point. Moses now would have a three-day lead on the pharaoh.

Finally they should meet somewhere in the next forty-eight hours. This means that all together Moses would be out approximately twenty-two days from Goshen before there would be any possibility whatsoever that Pharaoh and his troops would catch up with him.

A Different Scenario

One could paint a different scenario here. You could say that the pharaoh's armies moved at twice the speed of Moses. Even so, one gets approximately twelve to fifteen days for Moses to be outside of Egypt before the fateful meeting.

Traditional sources indicate that in addition to there being 600 of the finest chariots of Egypt, there were approximately 18,000 cavalry and about 80,000 foot soldiers, so the two-thirds pace is probably accurate.

For years there has been a cross-up on the Red Sea crossing. The cross-up is that people have assumed that the crossing took place three days outside of Goshen. By now you can see that is impossible.

Consider for a moment that even if Pharaoh's spies realized one day out that Moses was fleeing the country, it would have still taken them a day to get back to Pharaoh. Next, let's rush the time, saying it would take only one day to get ready (which seems unlikely), and a day to get back to where Moses was, you still have three days' time for Pharaoh to catch up to Moses. This would mean Moses must have been at least five, or perhaps as many as seven, days outside of Egypt prior to any encounter between the two of them.

Additional evidence that the crossing would have occurred more than three days out comes from Exodus 19:1–2, where we are told: "In the third month after the Israelites left the land of Egypt, the same day they came into the wilderness of Sinai . . . they encamped there before the mountain." It took Moses into the third month to get close to Mount Sinai.

The Bible is clear here; it took more than two months from leaving the land of Egypt to get to the base of Mount Sinai. If one accepts the traditional site, it is inconceivable that it would have taken over two months to travel that distance. After all, we are only talking about 130 miles.

Granted the terrain is difficult and barren. It would have been a laborious trip for Moses and his clan, but it certainly should not have taken three months to travel 130 miles, which comes to 1.4 miles a day. Play with the math of travel, any way you want. But one thing is certain, the Red Sea crossing has to be more than three days, and at the very minimum, five to seven days, outside of Goshen.

From Exodus 15 one can also get a sense of how far Mount Sinai is from the Red Sea crossing. The gist of the story here is that after the crossing Moses led the children of Israel away from the Red Sea crossing site three days (most authorities say this is thirty-three miles, which means they were traveling about eleven miles a day), into the wilderness and found no water. They came to Marah, where the water was bitter and could not be drunk. Moses turned the water sweet. They next went to Elim, where there were twelve springs of water and seventy palm trees, and camped by the waters.

The tribes still had not reached Mount Sinai. Chapter 16 hones in on the time frame of that a little bit more precisely and we are told: "They started out from Elim, and all the congregation of Israel came to the wilderness of Sin which is between Elim and Sinai, on the fifteenth day in the second month after they left the land of Egypt." Remember it took three months to get to Mount Sinai, fifteen days earlier they were at Elim, and they apparently arrived at Elim shortly after the crossing. My guess is about fifteen to twenty days after the Red Sea crossing. In short, Moses was a month and a half out of Goshen before coming close to Mount Sinai.

From this point, two time lines can be added to the Exodus. The Israelites started eating manna, but were told not to eat it on the seventh day. Some of them did, only to find that it had become filled with worms. Thus, they were in Elim at least seven days, which means they were almost two months outside of Egypt. Then the Israelites, according to Exodus 17, moved on to Sin by stages and encamped at Rephidim, which, as we know, is very close to Mount Sinai. This is where the battle of the Amalekites took place. So Mount Sinai must be at least *two months* outside of Goshen. The traditional Mount Sinai site is, by any stretch of the imagination, substantially closer than that.

We find agreement with our reasoning by U. Cassuto, who, translating from the Hebrew, uses references to new moons to conclude "we are now in the seventh week" when Moses arrives at the mountain.

Regardless of who you are, dear reader, you could walk from Cairo to the traditional Mount Sinai site in about fifteen days, assuming you are in reasonable shape. To traverse this distance in sixty days means you would be going less than two miles a day. Does that seem like the pace Moses would have chosen to flee Egypt?

"Yam-Sup"

Those who put forth the argument that the Red Sea crossing site was three or four days outside of Goshen find themselves beset with problems. The first of which is there is no Red Sea there. There is a Reed Sea, however, which some people claim to be the sea that Moses, through God's intervention, split in half so he and his followers could go through.

There is a great problem with this: the Reed Sea is a small body of water, certainly not deep enough to engulf and destroy Pharaoh's army of some 600 chariots and tens of thousands of others.

If it did take place there, and for some reason perhaps the sea was deeper then, remember, it is a lake, not an ocean or sea, and certainly the remnants of the crossing, particularly the 600 chariots which contained gold and bronze, would have been discovered. There has been no such discovery.

Numerous scholars of the Exodus have pointed out that *yam-sup* is the Hebrew word traditionally thought to mean the Red Sea. In fact, they claim it does not represent the Red Sea. Their view is that *yam-sup* translated from Hebrew means "Reed Sea." Because of this, a good many scholars and Sinai critics have considered for some time that the crossing took place at the Reed Sea, not the Red Sea. It was not until the writings of B. Batto, in *The Reed Sea: Requiescat in Peace,* that scholars began to reevaluate the Red Sea–Reed Sea problem.

The Reed Sea reference has always been to what's known as the Bitter Lakes about twenty miles north of the Gulf of Suez.

Translators have had a field day with the differences between

"Red" and "Reed" in determining which is the body of water Moses crossed.

Batto acknowledges that the Hebrew *sup* or *suph* refers to reeds or rushes, and probably could be translated into Sea of Papyrus of even Sea of Reeds.

An eleventh-century translator concluded that *yam-sup* refers to a marsh area where one will find reeds.

An interesting point with all authors who claim the crossing took place at the Reed Sea is that they mismatch their words. They continually talk about the Red Sea and then refer to the marsh area or Bitter Lakes. The difference is they call a sea, the Red Sea, just that, a sea. But then, in their own language, they refer to the Reed Sea as a marsh or lake.

A Lake or a Sea?

There is a difference between a lake and a sea. If that's the way we conceptualize them now, I suspect it was pretty much the same then. One does not use the same word for an ocean or a sea that one does for a lake. No one has argued about the word for "sea" in *yam-sup*; the only argument has been over red or reed.

That's not the issue though. The issue should be what type of body of water we are talking about. Are we talking about a lake or an ocean, a marsh or a sea? The specific use of the word "sea" is more compelling than "red" or "reed." Numbers 32:8 actually resolves this problem by telling us the Israelites "passed through the midst of the Sea."

If it was a lake, would not that word have been chosen and "sea" rejected?

Joshua 24:6 confirms this, saying, "I brought your fathers out of Egypt, and came to the *sea;* and the Egyptians pursued your fathers . . ." (emphasis added).

There are other Biblical references to the Red Sea that also pinpoint the area more specifically. I would refer you to First Kings 9:26 where we are told: "King Solomon made a fleet of ships in Eziongeber, which is beside Eloth, on the shore of the

Red Sea, in Edom." The reference is to the current town of Elot (also Eloth), on the northern edge of the Red Sea at the tip of the Gulf of Aqaba. It is due north of where Bob and I believe Moses made the crossing.

One might well ask, where did the coloring of the sea come from? Is the sea itself red?

No, it is not. It is one of the clearest, most beautiful waters one would ever have the pleasure of diving into. The waters here are impeccably clean, with no red coloring.

According to Dr. James K. Hoffmeier of Wharton College, the word *Edom* means "red," and while much of the land around the Gulf of Aqaba was controlled by the Edomites, the Israelites did not get along with them. Therefore, instead of calling it the Edomite Sea, the feud between these two tribes was tempered by naming this body of water the Red Sea instead.

This is certainly confirmed in Numbers 21:4 where we are told that Moses had "journeyed from Mount Horeb by the way to the Red Sea, to go around the land of Edom." Here again we have an Old Testament reference to the Red Sea. And note the reference to Edom, which can also be translated as red.

Hoffmeier also makes the point that if *sup* is related to the Egyptians, then perhaps *sup* refers to the end, such as the end of the stay in Egypt or the end of Pharaoh's army.

Another interesting point is made in Jeremiah 49:17; the reader is told that God has a plan against Edom that will be an "astonishment and shall hiss with horror at all its plagues and disasters."

We are told in verse 21: "At the sound of their fall, the earth shall tremble; at their crying, the sound shall be heard at the Red Sea." Again, a specific Red Sea reference, and close to Edom.

If you will refer again to a Biblical map, you will see that Edom is in the northern part of the Gulf of Aqaba. Thus, if something of some consequence were to occur there we doubt seriously it would be heard all the way to the Gulf of Suez, but it *would* be heard in the Gulf of Aqaba or the real Red Sea.

While we think there is good reason to believe that the crossing took place at the Straits of Tiran at the mouth of the Gulf of Aqaba, one could conclude that the crossing took place at the head of the Gulf of Aqaba. In fact, one needs to examine the entire length of the Gulf of Aqaba to Elot, even going into dry land on the assumption that perhaps the gulf has receded in the last few thousand years and put the crossing site on dry ground today.

There are so many Biblical references to Mount Sinai being in Midian, to Moses crossing the Red Sea (which is known from both the Old and New testaments to be the Gulf of Aqaba), that this is the area we believe serious Biblical researchers need to focus on for a crossing site and explain why there is no sign of the crossing on the Gulf of Suez branch of the Red Sea.

Too Steep

Topographical maps show that in the Gulf of Aqaba, as you can see in most cases, there is too sharp a dropoff for the Exodus tribe to have gone down into and up out of the Gulf of Aqaba basin, assuming for whatever reason the waters were split in half. It would have been an equally fantastic feat to lead men, women, children, dogs, and so forth down embankments of a thousand or more feet to then turn right back up and start climbing up similar, previously underwater hills prior to getting out of the seabed. The seabed is just too steep, both going in and going out, for an Exodus crossing at all places—with the exception of the Straits of Tiran or somewhere inland at the current head of the Gulf of Aqaba at Elat.

While several people argue that the Gulf of Aqaba has receded substantially since the Exodus crossing, an interesting point is that the Bible tells us there was a good deal of shipbuilding at Elat (or Elath). Shipbuilding still takes place there, as there is a deep harbor. If Elat were further north than where it is now, then one would need to find remnants of shipbuilding and some type of launching facility as well as a potential site for deep water. Topographical maps do not indicate that any such site could ever have existed. This is also confirmed by serious archaeological studies.

I'm sure you will agree with us by now that the traditional view of the Red Sea crossing simply doesn't jibe with reality.

It is interesting that Biblical scholars and archaeologists have not considered the backtracking the pharaoh's spies must have done to travel from Moses' camp back to Egypt, the preparation of the army, and the traveling from Egypt to wherever Moses had last been. It seems most scholars just assume that Moses went out three days and sat there waiting for the pharaoh.

This is not valid, however, when one considers the Biblical quotations indicating that Moses was provided with a light in front of him to travel at night and a cloud to follow during the day to aid his escape from Pharaoh. If God provided these things, then it certainly seems Moses would have used them. The Biblical Scriptures are clear on this one point: Moses knew he would be pursued by Pharaoh. Which means he must have had his people moving as fast as they could, "night and day," to get out from under Pharaoh's domain.

This view is reiterated in Exodus 14:20, where we are told: "Coming between the host of Egypt and the host of Israel . . . was a cloud and darkness to the Egyptians, but it gave light by night to the Israelites."

Now let's get on with the adventure of . . .

8.
Thy Kingdom Come

For six months I had been trying to get a visa into the Kingdom of Saudi Arabia, meeting with little success. Through a contact in London, Jack Trimonti, a fellow commodity trader, I was assured I'd be able to get in, because one of his friends "knew" one of the major princes of Saudi Arabia. I was given virtual assurance we would have "no problem" getting into the kingdom.

On my contact's word, I purchased tickets for Bob Cornuke and me from Los Angeles to New York, from New York to Jedda, Jedda to Tabuk, and on with the rest of our journey.

As countdown began, it became apparent that we were not getting our visas for Saudi Arabia. They were supposed to come, but didn't. Our sponsor's letter was supposed to arrive; it didn't. The day after that, a Federal Express package was supposed to arrive, but it didn't either.

I was getting antsy. Where were our visas? How would we get in? Finally, we received a fax, purporting to be from the king, which asked his government to grant us visas so we could do business in Riyadh.

The fax arrived in my California office Friday afternoon. Bob was driving from Colorado Springs the next morning. So I Federal Expressed the sponsor's letter to where he was staying; he then took our visa forms, pictures, and sponsor's faxed letter to the Saudi consulate in L.A. on Monday. We were scheduled to leave the next day around noon.

Turned Down

The Saudi consulate was quick to point out to Bob that this was just a faxed copy. It did not contain the king's signature. It was not received on their fax machine. Therefore, under no conditions or circumstances could it be accepted.

We immediately went into code red to see what could be done. The long and short of it is my contact in London said to come to London and we would work it out through the Saudi embassy there. That would be quicker and easier than working it through the Los Angeles consulate. The only way to do that was for me to catch a flight Monday afternoon out of San Diego about three o'clock. It was then eleven in the morning.

I finally got in touch with my wife, Carla, and told her to bring the kids home before she took them to the ballet classes, swimming lessons, and everything else, tied things up at the office as quickly as I could, rushed home, and began packing and seeing the kids. We had approximately two hours to do that before I had to be at the airport.

We called Jack to tell him what we were doing and he agreed it was the best idea. He would have his driver, Francis, pick us up the following morning.

At our London hotel we again told Jack of our problem, so he put us in touch with his Greek friend, Dimitrie, who shared an office with him. While most Greeks are neat and orderly, Dimitrie was large and overweight. Cigarette smoke lingered continually over his six-foot frame. He was a Grecian form of the American Babbitt, circa 1988. Dimitrie said "no problem"; he would get it done and we would be on our way the next morning.

We made dinner engagements with Jack. Jack showed us some English hospitality that night, taking us out to dinner with some of his clients to one of the gaming casinos, my first experience in a London casino. The gamblers were different from the ones in Las Vegas, quite a bit more subdued, yet each player was risking substantially more money than the average Las Vegas player. A heavy roller in our party lost about $70,000 that evening!

I am no big-time gambler. After all, why should I be? I trade commodities, and trading the market has treated me pretty well over the years.

The highlight of the evening was seeing America's most famous Greek, Telly Savalas, come into the casino and sit down to play blackjack at the 21 table. Even though I didn't go over to chat with him, Bob did and thought him a most congenial fellow.

We toasted the evening with assurances that we would be on our way to Jedda the following afternoon. But when the morning of what was supposed to be our last day in London unfolded, it became apparent we were not getting out of the country that day. Dimitrie's friend in the Saudi embassy apparently had forgotten his friendship, or Dimitrie did not have the clout he claimed.

We again took fax copies of the letter from the Saudi king requesting our admission, but the embassy would not take them, for the same reasons. They were fax copies. Now we really had a problem. The London embassy needed, by five o'clock that afternoon, a fax from the king in Saudi Arabia or we would not be allowed in the country.

The Fax of the Matter

Dimitrie, certainly one of the world's more creative Greeks, came up with a clever scheme. We went back to his office and programmed his fax machine to print out the king's phone number, time, everything, so that he could fax something (which he in fact did) to another fax machine in the U.S. to see if it would show any British identification, or if it would be traceable—in short, if it would appear to be a legitimate fax from the king. And that's what it appeared to be—a legitimate fax from the king. Dimitrie then faxed from his machine in London to the Saudi Arabian embassy, also in London, a fax that appeared to be legitimately from the king in Saudi Arabia.

Believe it or not the embassy went for it. They saw no problem with it at all and told us to come and give them some papers and passports. We were also given little stickers that said our passports would be ready Monday. But this was Thursday, we were supposed to be gone. That I didn't like. We had an official sticker that said the paperwork most likely would be processed, but nothing would be ready until Monday. I didn't want to spend that much time in London.

We decided to take Dimitrie out to dinner to put pressure on him to get the job done, to get us airborne quicker. I repeatedly urged him to make certain we would get our passports so we could be on a flight that left at noon the following day.

Dimitrie continued saying, "No problem, no problem." He had a friend in the Saudi embassy who would help. The friend was working at a casino, and would take care of him. I asked if I could advance money for this and he again said, "No, no problem," he would take care of it. In fact, Dimitrie told us that he would meet us at his office at ten in the morning. We would then go to the embassy, pick up our passports and visas, and be on our way.

Bob and I went to bed feeling good about what seemed to be, essentially, a done deal. Upon awaking, we found it was a slightly different matter. At ten there was no Dimitrie. Ten-fifteen, no Dimitrie. Ten-thirty, no Dimitrie. We decided the heck with Dimitrie, we would see what we could do on our own. Bob flagged a cab and we went to the Saudi embassy, the driver listening to our lament. When we got to the embassy, Bob went downstairs to see if our visas had been cleared.

The cab driver told me to get the receipts for our visas and passports from Bob and give them to him, because he, too, had a friend at the embassy. Our cab driver, whom we'll call Peter, did in fact have a friend at the embassy—something it appears Dimitrie never really had.

Peter took our receipts, gave them to his friend, and told us to wait. We were a bit skeptical, since that is what Dimitrie had been telling us for about three weeks. But who would you rather go with, the Greek or the cab driver? We took the cab driver. Peter, a dead ringer for Steve McQueen, was just as cool and efficient getting our passports as McQueen was driving that classic Mustang in the movie *Bullitt*.

Peter knew we had to catch a flight and so put more pressure on his friend in the embassy. We had approximately an hour and forty-five minutes to go, but no passports or visas in hand. I finally got Dimitrie on the phone. It sounded like he was waking up. He claimed he would be at the embassy in ten minutes. Ten minutes later there was no Dimitrie, but our cab driver winked. He had been given back our passports—and visas.

I called Dimitrie again, since he had our airline tickets. I reached him on his mobile phone and he said he was exactly two minutes from the embassy.

We waited exactly two minutes. No Dimitrie. Actually, we waited a grand total of three minutes and, knowing we had barely time to get to the airport, we told Peter, "Wheels up, let's go for it. We'll get new tickets issued at Heathrow."

Peter weaved and bobbed through London traffic like Sugar Ray Leonard in the late rounds of a fight. Bob and I were almost certain we would not make the plane. But we did, with twelve minutes to spare. Thanks, Peter!

And thanks to Dimitrie, for the creative use of a fax machine. We only hoped that this falsehood would not be detected and that we would be allowed to continue into the country, to get on with the business at hand.

My thoughts on the trip to the kingdom were as follows:

Would it be possible for two young men untrained in the ways of Biblical scholarship or archaeological research to document, locate, and establish that Mount Sinai is not in Egypt, but is instead in Saudi Arabia?

Realizing full well that it took more than an adventuresome spirit, something we unfortunately are possessed of, I knew we had to go beyond making this an adventure. We had to scientifically document our findings.

However, there was a problem. Neither of us has a great background in scientific investigation.

Sure, my companion and soul mate, Bob Cornuke, had been a member of the Costa Mesa Police Department S.W.A.T. team and had worked as an investigator for eight years. On that basis, Bob had scientifically investigated hundreds of murders and crimes. To that extent, Bob was used to dealing with measurements, establishing actual facts, and other details to hold up in a court of law.

That was just one of the advantages of having Bob along. Bob had also demonstrated on numerous occasions the ability to deal with violence, as well as with monolithic bureaucracies.

A stocky former college football star, Cornuke is the type of guy you do not want to tangle with, in or out of uniform, not just because of his size, but because of his speed.

I recall my first ill-fated competition with him, a race along the shores of the Red Sea in Egypt, approximately four months earlier. I thought I could beat him, despite being almost ten years older. I'm certain I could beat him in a longer distance, because that is my strength, but when it comes to short, quick sprints, Bob Cornuke is one fast man.

Shortly after the race, while basking in the sun-drenched Straits of Tiran, Bob and I discussed what a couple of fellows could do to a community as small as the one we were gazing over.

He said, "You'd be surprised, with my police training it would take about six guys and we could have total control of this town in less than twelve hours."

He is blessed with a sense of humor as well. The contradiction of Bob Cornuke is that in sharp contrast to his toughness he has strong Christian faith.

My scientific pursuits have been in trying to figure out how to beat the stock and commodity markets, something I began to do in the mid 1960s. Thanks to some decent research, a little bit of luck, and good timing, I have been able to parlay a small amount of money into a nest egg of sorts. While it may be true that money can't buy happiness, it can certainly buy adventure, time, and experiences. And that's what my money was doing on this trip—buying something bigger than beating the market.

While I'm no stranger to computers and scientific methods, it certainly is not my basic nature. I started as an art major in college and quickly switched to journalism because I wasn't good enough as an artist yet still wanted to communicate something in some way.

On the plane I kept asking myself if this wasn't just one gigantic ego communication to the world, to attempt to document something that no one has done in the last 4,000 years—to prove that Mount Sinai is not where the majority of people think it is.

One needs to be careful about the pursuit of adventure. Not only is it a will-o'-the-wisp ego trip, it also causes you to lose a bit of your rational senses. Because you focus on the goal, the target, not the impossibility of getting to the goal or the target.

Frankly, my goal was simple. I wanted to establish the true site where Moses crossed the Red Sea, and the true Mount Sinai.

That it had not been done was not my concern. I'm used to treading where others fear.

As an example, for years, college professors have sat on their duffs, smoked pipes from stuffy armchairs, and said that the market is not predictable—stocks or commodities. My research indicated they were not just a little wet, but flat-out wrong. That the professorial types were wrong in an area as simple to research and evaluate as stocks and commodities made me wonder about archaeological discoveries.

Not that I don't have respect for the Groves of Academe, I do, a great deal. Had it not been for my college training (B.S., University of Oregon), I would not have been able to accomplish the few things I have.

It strikes me, though, that the big things, the "impossible dreams," are not envisioned by the educational system. What that takes is hard work, a little bit of cash, and some decent research to pull off things that most people think can't be done.

Throbbing away in my thoughts was the possibility that we would find the true Mount Sinai. It would have all the qualifying factors, as mentioned in Biblical literature, but still would not get accepted by the scientific and religious community because of our background. That, in turn, put more pressure —which was fine—on us to do it right, to make certain we didn't screw it up along the way.

Twice already our potential site had proven difficult to document. My friend David Fasold and Ron Wyatt stumbled across the site which Fasold validated. About a year earlier Wyatt, by himself, tried to get to the site. In both instances, they ended up in jail and were not able to leave with any evidence, other than their stories, as to what lay at the foot of the mountain.

The way I saw it was as follows. Fasold and Wyatt had an idea where the fish were—Fasold, who may well have discovered the real Ark of Noah in Turkey (see *The Ark of Noah*, Wynwood Press), with his electronic measuring tools, and natural yen to dig and uncover the truth, was able to spot some fish and say, "Indeed they are there." However, neither he nor Wyatt was able to bring the fish home.

I was flying to Saudi Arabia to catch some fish in the desert. The archaeological trophies of the Red Sea crossing and Mount Sinai play off each other. If you can establish where the Red Sea crossing was, you have a decent idea where Mount Sinai should be. By the same token, if you can positively establish where Mount Sinai is, you have drawn a direct bead on where the Red Sea crossing took place.

Most current archaeologists and mapmakers, in my opinion, as you know, have gone on a wild goose chase, saying that the true Mount Sinai is on the Egyptian peninsula.

My mind kept saying it just wasn't so. The traditional crossing sites most people have accepted are based not on archaeology, but either on a sixteenth-century mystic who claimed she had a revelation where the crossing was, or on Biblical scholars. In both instances, there is a good deal of geological information indicating that the crossing could not have taken place in the western branch of the Red Sea, the Gulf of Suez.

Other Red Sea Crossing Sites

There are two primary reasons why those crossing sites are wrong. First, the crossing sites that have been proposed by most people are too wide. In one instance, it would be approximately fifteen miles across the Red Sea, and in another it would be almost thirty miles across. Yet the Bible, which one must assume to be true if you go along with the rest of the Red Sea story, tells us Moses and the tribe crossed in the nighttime, and by morning were out. They had anywhere from seven to nine hours, with a bare minimum of 100,000 people, and perhaps as many as 30,000 animals, to cross the sea in that time. Most likely, though, Moses led over half a million people—there's no way you could move that many thirty, or even fifteen miles in such a short time over even flat, dry land.

Second, the geological structure, as examined through topographical maps of the bottom of both branches of the Red Sea, shows precipitous descents of almost a thousand feet at the traditional Red Sea crossing sites—essentially, the Exodus group would have been jumping off a cliff to make the crossing. You may wish to study the topographical map, which will validate our thinking as well as indicate what would appear to be the most logical crossing site.

Also, the traditional crossing sites do not have a stone or rock bottom, and the Bible says they crossed on dry land, yet geological studies show that from time immemorial the crossing sites lay over forty to sixty feet of mud!

Propelled by the Saudi airline's finest 747, we knew that in about seven hours we should be landing in the kingdom. This was a major event in our lives, something we had waited and worked for for a long time. I had tried for almost half a year just to get into the country.

We knew life in the kingdom would be different from anything in America. We had been told numerous stories by our few friends who had been there, and they had outlined basically what we should expect. Of course, everyone had warned us about the inadvisability of what we were doing, for ending up in jail as other would-be archaeologists had was a real possibility.

But being optimistic and good-natured people, we just never dwelled on what could happen to us. Or that, if anything did, we would, in some fashion, be able to extricate ourselves from any situation.

We knew we would have a long and tiring trip ahead of us, so we used our time aboard the plane for as much rest and relaxation as possible. We ate what we knew would be the last decent, or at least recognizable, food. Airline food is far from the best in the world, yet compared to what we were about to have, it would be longingly remembered.

We did have one lingering worry and that was what would happen when we tried to get into the country. What information would be at the check-through points? Would they have investigated our fax from the king? Would they find out it was bogus?

Entering the Kingdom

Deboarding the plane at Jedda was just about the same as deboarding any plane in any international terminal—that means you are confronted with lines to show your passports, present your papers, and have your baggage checked.

I summoned up all the courage I had as I stepped forward to be checked through, handing my passport to a young man (all of eighteen or nineteen) who was not only carefully scrutinizing people's passports but also their faces and how they looked. Would we make it through?

As I stepped up to the counter, Bob gave me a smile. I

shrugged my shoulders, winked back, and took a deep breath—it was time to be cool.

The opening lines of a hymn drifted through my head: "Turn back, O man, forswear thy foolish ways. Old now is earth and none may count her days."

I gave the uniformed, gun-toting guard my passport and visa. He key-punched my numbers into a computer. The moment of truth was near . . .

In some fashion, however, everything in the computer was correct, because the policeman was eventually able to access the data, fill it in, and, lo and behold, I was in. I said Bob was my partner and that we had the same sponsor, so he was also breezed through.

The next point was to get our luggage cleared through customs. It started as "no problem" at all. We were the last in line and I'm certain the customs agent was tired of looking through bags, poking around dirty underwear, and who knows what else people were carrying in their luggage.

Everything was smooth sailing until I opened up my video camera, one of the super-small type. That immediately brought the agent's attention to my gear. He started asking questions about the videotapes. I told him, "There is nothing on it. They are blank. Perhaps there are pictures of my wife and daughter playing their harps." That, however, wasn't good enough. He took the tapes and told me to sit down. I asked why. He said to please sit down.

Again I asked why, and he again told us to please, sit down. My tapes were taken; and about five minutes later someone came back and said in broken English, "Are you the one with the camera?" I said yes. He said, "Come with me."

I walked back through the immigration control point that I had already cleared, and around the offices and cubicles until I came to the one I dubbed the "grand inspector" of all videos.

This chap had my videos and wanted to talk to me about them. He also pointed out that he did not have the correct equipment for viewing them, so would I go back and get my camera so he could look at them. I turned around (he had my passport) and brazenly walked through the visa checkpoint. To think that just a few minutes before I had been scared to death to walk through there, and now I simply opened up the gate, walked over to my luggage, picked up my camera, and came back—the same process without anyone saying as much as boo to me on this unescorted trip.

Back in the great videotape censor's office, I found him more interested in the Arabic television show he was watching than in my film. There was nothing on my three tapes so he had to fast forward, rewind, and fast forward several more times to try to find something on them. He was certainly in no hurry.

As he was doing that, I glanced around the room to see what types of things they had confiscated. It was hard to tell, since they were in various types of boxes. Some were not marked. Others were obviously videos people tried to sneak in, with titles on the boxes such as *Alice in Wonderland, Rocky, The Sound of Music,* and a few other nondescript titles. I doubt there was anything offensive with the titles—just what people dubbed on them.

Here we were at ten or eleven o'clock at night, with someone I judged to be about twenty-five years old, and he was the sole censor of videotapes coming into the country.

What type of person was this? How was he selected? Was he chosen because he was the most antiprurient person in the country? What an interesting job to have, looking at people's home movies and actual copies of movies to occasionally find material to censor. A far cry from America's print-anything attitude.

Once he was satisfied my tapes were blank, he was kind enough to give my passport back. Away we went.

Saying "away we went" isn't quite correct. We stayed in the same airport for about three hours, awaiting our flight to Jedda. Around midnight, both Bob and I dozed off, taking a quick twenty-minute catnap, which was the only type of sleep we had been getting the last few days.

Boarding the flight to Jedda was easy. We had learned to clear the innumerable checkpoints and took them in stride. The flight went well until we were told to "buckle your seat belts and return the tray table to the upright and locked position." From that point on, we spent the next forty-five minutes circling. It got to the point where Bob and I took out our compasses to see how many circles we were making.

Since I was sitting next to the window, I could see from the air that Tabuk was not a large town. Probably some 20,000 to 30,000 people at most. And I should know, since I got four distinct views of it as we kept circling overhead. On the fifth circle, I told Bob I thought something was wrong. The more we studied the situation, the more we agreed either the landing wheels did not go down or there was a problem with the flaps. We continued making a large circle over the desert. I suspected the pilot was dumping fuel.

Finally we proceeded to our landing. It was an extremely long approach when suddenly we dropped from the skies onto the tarmac. It was like a pogo stick. We just plopped down with a loud bang, bounced up, only to be slammed back down.

Bob immediately said, "I think we blew a tire."

I wasn't certain, but it was obvious we had had a bad landing and something was wrong. As we started to taxi in, I called Bob's attention to the fire engines on the runway. He counted thirteen trucks awaiting our arrival. There seemed to be no great urgency to escort us off the plane, so I assumed there was no great problem, just one of those shaky landings you prefer not to have.

One nice thing the Saudi airline does is read one of Mohammed's prayers prior to takeoff. I was glad we had one on this trip!

We asked our flight attendants what had happened and they wouldn't tell us. They just said, "Oh, nothing, no problem." (Now, whenever I hear the phrase "no problem," believe me, I get worried.) When we assured them we wouldn't tell anyone what happened, they started to open up a little but only gave us clues.

Down on the ground, Bob and I checked the tires, which were still intact, although the left front one looked like it had made its last landing. We finally got one of the attendants to talk with us and he said the flaps were not working.

Bob and I felt we had enough surprises and alarms for one day and were ready to go to our hotel. We got our luggage and were relieved to find there were no more baggage inspection points. Apparently, we had passed all the security that we were going to encounter—at least for a while.

We caught a cab and started toward our hotel, the Tabuk Sahara.

On the way we saw numerous groups of people. Some looked like families (all this at about 2:30 to 3:00 in the morning) with their cars, having what appeared to be picnics alongside the road. It certainly seemed to be a strange time for family outings. I told Bob I thought these people were part bat! It seemed that each time friends in London called the Saudis, they were told they were taking a nap. It didn't matter whether it was morning, noon, or night, someone always seemed to be taking a nap in that country.

One of the things that Bob pointed out to me is that Saudis are not big on working, especially physical work. This seems to permeate their society. At the airport you see Koreans, Japanese, and Chinese sweeping the floors, serving people, doing the tasks that are necessary to maintain the airport.

Our cab driver was from Manila, as was the hotel attendant who checked us in.

They say there is very little crime in Saudi Arabia. That is usually ascribed to the stiff penalties. There might be another reason: there is simply no darkness here.

As we drove in from the airport, we must have passed at least 40,000 streetlights. If there is a street, and if there is a building, it is well illuminated.

The Saudis are obviously oblivious to any energy crisis. It looks like they want to add to it by burning up as much fossil fuel as they can now, to stimulate higher prices later on. We passed one set of lights on the highway that would have made Times Square seem small-town. The only thing that was missing was the theaters and the nightlife.

Instead, there was nothing, just desert and a divided road. The lights weren't there for anything we could ascertain other than to burn up oil and "beautify" the night scenery.

As I looked out my hotel window, I could see only two moving cars. By then it was four in the morning, but I could count directly in front of me over 150 streetlights on two roads. My visibility was approximately one mile. The night was awash in orange, firefly-like lights, surrounding us like candles on a birthday cake.

Friday, June 10, 1988

One could not ask for a more accommodating hotel than the Tabuk Sahara. The next day, sitting near a fifty-foot-long, turquoise-green swimming pool, my thoughts drifted back to the previous night's entry to Jedda.

Jedda had the weather I expected—hot, muggy, and uncomfortable, weather that climbs onto you and doesn't leave, doesn't leave while you walk the streets, doesn't even leave the sheets that cling to you at night. You always have the sense of the heat being out there. A sense there is a battle going on outside the air-conditioned rooms between you and the elements.

Tabuk, however, was quite the opposite. The night we arrived it greeted us with a pleasant, balmy evening, the type of evening that brings back thoughts of younger years walking with the love of your life in a city park, swinging on swings. It was just that pleasant.

The next day turned out to be equally pleasant. It is certainly warmer than in the States, but we were not overwhelmed by the heat that drives one to lethargy.

We saw no native people working. Of course, the types of workers we encountered were cab drivers, cooks, waiters, hotel desk clerks, a physical therapist/lifeguard at the pool. The vast majority of these people are from the Philippines and seem to be relatively pleased. They sign on for a two-year contract, and make substantially more money than they would back home. Their English is much better than that of most of the Saudis, and they all have pleasant dispositions, which must help in their jobs.

The first morning we were joined for breakfast by a Dutchman and a Saudi who had been educated at Monterey Peninsula Community College and Iowa State University.

We shared thoughts as well as food for about an hour and learned a good deal about the country.

The thing that had been worrying Bob the most was snakes, so his first question to the Saudi was about snakes. We were assured there were none in this part of the kingdom. Bob liked the answer. Yet every night he spent on the desert, he was careful to sleep well off the ground, usually on the seat of our rented truck.

A Friday to Remember

It was Friday in Saudi Arabia, which is comparable in some ways to what Sunday used to be in the United States: a day of rest. We went out that morning to try to buy provisions for our escapade, making it to the store about half an hour before closing time, which is high noon, when prayer begins.

The first and largest store we came to was already closed. The second store was in the process of closing and scooted us out. We had just enough opportunity to buy a flashlight, water to last us two or three days, and a watermelon.

While everything else seemed so modern, the grocery store where we purchased our first round of supplies was more reminiscent of Mexico or Egypt than what I expected to find in Saudi Arabia.

The town of Tabuk looks very much like Lebanon did before the war. The buildings are cement, some of which have been splashed with color. But the color selection ranges from unfinished concrete gray to white, with a few speckled with turquoise, indicating the owner of that building has been to Mecca for his once-in-a-lifetime trip.

Back home in the States, as well as in London, I had been

told that their Friday was like our Sunday, a total shut-down day, that nothing would be open. That was not quite the case. What actually happens is the stores are open from about ten in the morning until eleven-thirty, and shut down for prayer time, which lasts from twelve to three. Stores then resume opening anywhere from three-thirty to four, and will stay open until six, when it is again time to turn East in prayer. They then open again for an hour or two in the evening.

Our intentions were to get the rest of our provisions and be gone the next morning. We initially thought we could make it on our first day. But thinking about it, we decided that would be foolish. We were still too tired from our London problems, and both of us still suffered what we hoped was not a terminal case of jet lag. Offsetting the jet lag was our desire to get out and start digging, to uncap, unscrew, and photograph whatever was there.

We spent the last three hours going over the treatises we had brought with us, including the Bible, trying to again decipher what the facts of the situation were, what should be apparent at Mount Sinai and what should not be. There were some things that definitely should be there and we jotted them down before we started our trip.

One thing for certain, we knew the next day we would be out of Tabuk and into the terrible wilderness, or the desert area, where Jabal al Lawz is situated.

We spent the afternoon soaking up the sun, a little bit of swimming, and a whole lot of orange juice before turning in early. We had the good fortune to be able to rent a Datsun pickup, and finished outfitting ourselves well for the trip.

By the time the sun had set, we had acquired flashlights, shovels, brooms for sweeping off artifacts, plenty of water, and fresh fruit and vegetables, as well as canned goods that we felt would last us through just about anything. This was in addition to Bob's backpacking food in tinfoil packs.

We had also brought with us things you would expect—compasses, binoculars, rope, measuring instruments, cameras, tape recorders for dictation, everything you can think of to adequately and fully document whatever lay in front of us.

In the hotel we hashed and rehashed, not only what to look for, but what our plan of attack would be so we would catch the fish, not have the fish catch us. The rest of that afternoon, like professional chess players, we set out the possibilities, then planned our offensive and defensive strategies. We tested each other in an effort to make certain this trip would not fail due to poor planning or not anticipating the obvious. By the evening we knew we were ready for the action to begin.

Yes, sleep came easily that night. But on the way there were a lot of questions, a lot of thoughts rambling around in my mind. The most lingering thought was that answers to many of these questions were about to unfold in front of us as we would soon be . . .

9.
Going to the
Mountain

Our First Trip

Even though we had a wake-up call for five the morning of
June 10, 1988, we were out of bed long before the call came, and
by six we were on the road, following David Fasold's instructions and my topographical map. We soon found ourselves at
the Al Kan gas station and things looked easy. However, that
would change quickly.

According to David's instructions we should find a turnoff
four kilometers past the gas station. Unfortunately we did not.
We drove up and down the road several times looking for a
road to turn south, to our left, but could not find any such road
so went back to the gas station to replay our maps.

Let me digress a bit about the gas stations in Saudi Arabia.
They are certainly not like the 7-Elevens or Conoco stations
back home. The main difference is they are incredibly dirty. If
you were to go inside the station you would not want to touch
anything, not even the change you get back. There are almost
always no paved parking areas at the pumps.

Gas is relatively expensive. To fill up the Datsun pickup took about fifteen U.S. dollars. (I should point out that in Saudi Arabia a fill-up doesn't really mean a fill-up. Every time we asked for people to fill up our tank, we only got about three-quarters of a tank. And there's no unleaded gas—Detroit still has a market for cars without catalytic converters and it's in Saudi Arabia.)

Finally we had no choice but to take the only thing that appeared to be a road. We were looking for something of consequence, something that you could easily drive upon. What we found was a mere hint, a whisper of a trail winding through sand. The only thing that made us feel good about the trail we found is that it appeared to wander in the general direction we thought we should go.

Once we left the paved road we were on the floor of a large desert valley and began to pick our way carefully between rocks, gullies, sand drifts, sagebrush, and cactus.

Our Southwest is rough, but not nearly as rough and jagged or as dry and uninhabitable as the Saudi desert.

We attempted to follow David's meticulous instructions to the letter. The first thing we were to look for was a large outcropping at 8.0 kilometers, another one at 16.8 kilometers, and a set of tower rocks to our left at 22.4 kilometers.

Frankly, though, we couldn't see any of what had been so obvious to David. We just kept bouncing along trusting we were going in the right direction. That is all we knew. We had a general direction to go in and hoped at some point we might run across someone who could point out the mountain to us or that we could define it from the topographical map.

Along the way to the mountain we saw a good deal of activity, much more than we thought we would see in the desert. I didn't think we would see anyone out there in that forsaken place.

In fact, there were all kinds of people out there on our way to the mountain that morning. We saw people herding camels. We saw a herd of wild camels. We saw several Bedouin camp-sites each comprising five to ten small trucks, tents, and thousands of sheep.

Stuck in the Desert

At one point we decided to turn around. Perhaps we had gone in the wrong direction. Bob pulled off the road to make the turn and we were immediately stuck in the sand—up to the axles. First, we tried digging out but the endless sand caved in making it worse. Miles from nowhere, we were hopelessly stuck. The more we spun the tires, the deeper we sank into the sand. We jammed sagebrush, small rocks, anything, under the wheels to try to get out. Nothing worked. By then some Bedouins, three men and seven or eight young boys, appeared on the scene and, true to their friendly nature came over to help.

The Bedouins immediately took the rocks and sagebrush out from under the tires and told us to rock the truck back and forth instead. We did that, and as the sand slipped under our tires due to the lifting, rocking motion, the truck raised itself up and we were freed from our dilemma in no time.

We gave oranges to the young lads as our sincere appreciation, and they slowly peeled those succulent fruits, savoring each juicy bite. The children were as pleased to get those oranges as American children on Christmas morning.

Since our cover had been penetrated and our identity exposed, at least to some extent, we asked these people how to find Ibraham Frich, the local Bedouin who tends most of the sheep in this great valley.

We finally broke the language barrier and got the point across that we would like to go to Frich's camp. We wanted to see Frich for two reasons. First, we wanted to tell him hello from David and to give him some things we had bought for him in town that we thought perhaps he would like. Second, David told us that Frich's camp was right at the base of Jabal al Lawz, so we would not have to ask where the mountain was.

We finally got one of the Bedouins to agree to take us to Frich's camp, so we followed behind his truck through the desert for about another twenty-five minutes.

We turned eastward up a large, flat ravine, about three-quarters of a mile wide and apparently endless. We then followed our lead driver into a campsite, complete with camels, three tents, lots of scurrying children, a couple of mangy barking dogs, and some sheep sleeping in a huddled group under the shade of tents.

Our trail guide got out of his pickup and walked over to one of the tent areas where someone was sleeping. He gently woke the person up and asked where Frich was. We were told he was in Tabuk, shopping, and would not be back until later in the day, about four or five in the afternoon. He suggested we wait for Frich to return.

Asking Got the Wrong Answer

That was not to our liking since we aren't the type of guys to sit around all day. It was now about eleven o'clock in the morning and that would have been a long time for us to sit on our hands. We decided to ask our Bedouin guide to take us to Jabal al Lawz.

That was a mistake!

Our request altered the Bedouin's mood. He first said he couldn't do it; he gave the impression we shouldn't go there, said it was not an area for us to go to. Since we were now confused about our directions, we didn't have any other choice but to press the issue a little further.

The Bedouin finally took us but was leery about going to the site. When we got to the base of the mountain, instead of just getting out of his pickup truck and showing us the mountain, he pulled out his binoculars and cautiously slid around a point of rocks. He stood, eyed something in the distance, then came back to us and motioned for us to follow him. He got back in his pickup; we followed and could not believe what we saw.

We had found David's reference point: a large "balanced rock," a mountain with two stones on the top with a large tree between them—what may be Mount Sinai—Jabal al Lawz.

The shocker was that a huge fence had been built around the entire base of the mountain. The government had fenced off approximately 200 acres and there was a large sign, white on blue, in English and Arabic, that said "No Trespassing Allowed." This was an area the Minister of Antiquities had set apart. The fence was approximately fifteen feet high with barbed wire at the top. Clearly, Fasold's find had been acknowledged by the Minister of Antiquities of Saudi Arabia, and now it was off-limits.

There we were. We had finally located the mystery site out in the middle of the Saudi desert but were unable to get inside.

According to David's description there should be petroglyphs on rocks to the south of the area. We would go try to find them. The Bedouin thought otherwise, telling us to follow him. He motioned, telling us to stop taking pictures. We followed him back down a road. We weren't sure where we were going, but he made certain we were following him. When we slowed up, he slowed up. When we stopped, he stopped and waved us to come to him.

Finally, he stopped next to a large wadi in front of a building that looked to our inquiring minds to be a prison, a jail, or some sort of government structure.

We were more than a little anxious to see what was going to take place next. Earlier the Bedouin had written down our license plate number, which caused us both concern. Now all the authorities had to do was check car rental agencies and we were done for.

Our Bedouin went inside the building to return with a white-robed gentleman who spoke much more English than our Bedouin. That still wasn't very much. We were able to establish a couple of things, though: that this was some type of school and they wanted our passports.

We played as dumb as possible at that point, which was not difficult. When they pronounced the word "passport," they pronounced it "puss pro." We pretended not to understand and kept saying "hotel, hotel" to them, hoping that perhaps they thought our passports were at the hotel.

Next, we were instructed not to take any more photographs until we went back to Tabuk and got our passports.

We then said, "Oh, passports! Passports! We have our passports. We didn't know that's what you wanted." We went to our car and got our passports, so they saw we were "legitimate" and did have visas to get into the country. They now seemed satisfied with our being there. In addition, Bob quickly scrounged through his gear and found our invitation letter to visit the country from the king, the letter Dimitrie had created on his fax machine in London.

This seemed to really impress the white-robed fellow, who talked with the Bedouin, explaining what our papers meant. They invited us to come back at four in the afternoon to have tea with them. We said we would and thanked them very much for getting us unstuck and showing us Jabal al Lawz. Things seemed to be going well after all.

After further inquiry we found that this was a school David had mentioned in his notes to me. He had also said to make sure we didn't go down to it. Well, here we were. Not only had we gone to it, but they had written down our passport numbers as well as our license plate number. Who knew what evil things would befall us here in the desert. I didn't know, but I'll tell you, Bob and I had all sorts of visions of things lurking around in the desert, and we started to get our first case of gun-shyness.

Soon we bade them adiós and headed back up to Jabal al Lawz to see what we could see. In particular we wanted to see if we could find the petroglyphs David had mentioned. We found a place where we could park the truck out of sight from anyone who would be traveling on the road up the large valley floor. I went north and Bob went south in pursuit of petroglyphs. I thought for certain that I had located the rocks David talked about.

Finding the Altar of the Golden Calf

He said there was a small basin where water collected on top of one of the large rocks, and there was a large crack on the right-hand side of this. I thought I had found the structure but could not find any drawings, no Egyptians, no cows, no stick figures of men.

I spent almost an hour looking all over the rock outcroppings in the area, checking every one of them. Much to my disappointment, there wasn't anything there. I couldn't even conjure or twist something to look like something else. It simply wasn't there.

Eventually, I started heading back toward the car, only to hear Bob yell, shouting my name several times. I gave a short, sharp whistle back and went on a dog trot. I soon saw him, as I got on top of a knoll. I waved and Bob returned the wave, giving me a thumbs-up sign, yelling that he had found it.

What he had found was not what I was expecting. He had found the large group of rocks David had mentioned. But this area also had been secured by the kingdom with a security fence about fifteen feet high, with barbed wire at the top and a large blue sign which I photographed. This sign was a repeat of what we had seen at the base of Jabal al Lawz, telling readers it was protected by the Minister of Antiquities, there were serious fines, you were not to go inside, and you were not to take photographs. Again, it was in English and Arabic and the message was clear: this area is off-limits.

Peering through the fence, though, we could easily see the petroglyphs of the bulls and what we believe could be the altar site of the golden calf.

I still wasn't firmly convinced this was the real Mount Sinai, or the rock outcropping was the altar site of Aaron. However, one thing was starting to shape up pretty well. There were some unusual anomalies at the base of this large mountain in the midst of the Saudi desert. They looked out of place, and the kingdom, for some reason, had fenced this area off at some expense. Certainly, they think something of importance is here. And we knew their archaeology professors had been on the site.

After photographing the petroglyphs at the rock site, we took more pictures looking up to the mountain and back through the valley where we had been. We then hopped in the pickup, driving west about a half a mile. Then things really started to hit me. I did not discuss this with Bob. But what I saw convinced me that this was the place where it was most possible and most logical for Moses and his tribes to have gathered.

Why? Because there was an abundant amount of sagebrush and grass, green trees and flowers. There are wonderful camping sites. Certainly enough room to hold 600,000 or more people on this plateau of what we know in the American West as high chaparral country. The most important thing missing at all the other Mount Sinai locations, enough camping space, was more than abundant here.

Seeing a road bearing off down to the right that might take us closer to the base of the mountain, Bob and I maneuvered the truck down to that area. As we were bouncing around, I noticed a rock with petroglyphs to our left. We stopped the truck and started taking photographs.

We suspected we shouldn't be taking photographs, and we wondered if the schoolteacher Dave had warned us about or the Bedouin had given our license plate number to the police, who would soon be out to nab us. We just didn't know. All we knew is that we had to move in—move in quickly, get as much as we could, and get the heck out of there.

A Picture of Worship

Apparently the government or Minister of Antiquities had not seen these petroglyphs that I found to the south side of the road that goes to the base of the mountain, as they were not fenced off. What they show is interesting. They are not nearly as good drawings of the Egyptian bull, but they do show people holding the bull over their heads, as if honoring or worshiping.

This is striking evidence that a long time ago something fascinating took place at the base of this mountain. This special symbol that someone embedded on these rocks thousands of years ago appears to recount some type of sacred relationship between the man and the bull.

As we got farther down this road, we started to drop down a ravine as we approached the base of the mountain, where we were once again confronted by the security fence blocking off the base of Jabal al Lawz.

We stared out over the fence for a long, sorrowful minute. We had come so close—almost halfway around the world— only to be stopped by a fence. But what could we do? The signs made it clear. The experiences of David and Ron also made it clear that one should not mess with Saudi antiquities.

So we got back in the pickup and proceeded south and slightly west. There is a large passageway in this valley that comes up to the spot where the petroglyphs are. We worked down this valley, which would be basically the direction in which Moses would have brought his people if, in fact, the Red Sea crossing is at the Straits of Tiran. This valley is broad, it's wide, and it, too, is verdant, at least with sagebrush and scrub plants. There are numerous rock canyons along the side of this larger canyon to suggest water has run in the past or runs now. We saw a good number of beautiful green trees.

We went another two miles down this valley, seeing as much as we could, stopping to see if there were more petroglyphs or signs, but we saw none. What we did see, though, appeared to be stone graves or markers. We did not dig the graves to see what was under them, but it certainly did appear that there are people buried out there and that some of these sites are mass graves. There are large piled-up stone mounds—certainly too large to be sheepherder monuments.

Turning around and driving back toward the petroglyphs at the base of the mountain, it really all came together for me. You could almost feel the twelve tribes of Israel working their way through here, getting to this spot to rest.

The most demonstrable evidence to me continued to be the bulls, the drawings. Especially significant was that they appeared in no place other than the high rock altarlike outcropping that could easily be seen from the mountain we believe could be Mount Sinai. In the two-and-a-half-mile jaunt down the valley we saw no petroglyphs. We looked long and hard to see if any were there, but there were none. Leaving the valley at the other end, we also looked for petroglyphs or signs of drawings, but again, nothing was there. The only signs we saw were in two places: one, which looked like a ceremonial outcropping of rocks, where the majority of petroglyphs are, and the other, slightly west and south of that spot, approximately halfway between the big petroglyph outcropping, and prior to the base of the mountain.

It looked like it was time to leave the entire site, camp for another run at it the next day, go down to our four o'clock tea appointment at the school, or drive back to Tabuk and try to leave the country as soon as possible.

We had done nothing wrong. All we had done was to take pictures. But we were so spooked by the government of Saudi Arabia and the vague uncertainty of their laws and what they were known to do to people that paranoia began to settle upon us.

About four kilometers away from the base of the mountain, Bob brought up the very good point that we had not taken any pictures with my video camera. So, reaching for my VHS, we turned back one more time to shoot the area, capturing the three mountains which have, I think, the most impressive vantagepoint. After all, mountains look pretty much like mountains. But such a large valley at the base of the mountain certainly fits what was supposed to have taken place at Mount Sinai, topography that simply does not exist at any other sites.

Inside the Fence

Once we were back at the base of the mountain, I looked at Bob and said, "As long as we have come this far, let's see if we can't get inside the fence. Let's take one shot at it to see if we can't find the twelve pillars of Moses that David said are at the base of the mountain, as well as other physical structures that should be there."

We set our binoculars on the fenced-off area to see what it looked like. It appeared we had one of two options: either to run up around the end of the fence where it dead-ended into the side of the mountain, or to try to dig a hole and shimmy our way underneath the fence at a low point in a ravine.

We opted for the latter choice as it would give a more direct route to where we wanted to go. We decided that I would do it; I would run in, snap a photo of this mysterious valley, and be out in seconds.

I knew I was taking a huge risk penetrating the fence. I thought about it for a little bit and decided it was well worth it. I don't know if I was frightened or thrilled. My feeling was, Let's get on with it; let's see what's back there.

Bob stayed behind (underneath some rocks where we were certain he would not be seen) so in the event something happened to me at least he would be safe and could bail me out. I meandered casually down to the fence, kind of looking it over. Once I got close to it, it became apparent that digging underneath it was the best way to proceed, since the fence in that particular spot goes across the old creek that comes out of the canyon from the north side of Jabal al Lawz. Where it crosses the fence there is no dirt but an amalgamation of sand and gravel. It was easy to dig a crawl space maybe ten inches deep underneath the fence, put my camera inside the perimeter, then squirm through the hole to the other side.

Once inside the fence, there was no more meandering. It was time to make a go for it, so I blasted across the flat space as quickly as I could, looking for some type of cover. It was a long way off, so I had to run to the best of my ability. I was bouncing along, looking to see if anyone else was back there, as well as trying to find the sites that David Fasold had talked to me about.

Initially I didn't see anything at all. Then I ran up a draw on top of some rocks to get a vantage point. I was looking due east, and not seeing anything, when out of the corner of my eye I caught the reflection of a pickup truck. I instantly ducked down to get cover and to get a better look at the truck to see if

I had been spotted. The truck was there all right, but it had no tires: it had been abandoned—junked.

I was on my way. I continued picking my way across rock piles and into little wadis, looking for pillars, outcroppings, petroglyphs, anything that would indicate that somebody had done something back here.

A small hill appeared in front of me, so I crawled up on my belly to peek over to see what was there. Then I saw what I didn't want to see. Off in the distance (where I now know an altar or temple site is), I saw a few Bedouins standing, looking over the valley. I could clearly see the Bedouin garb blowing in the wind. Again my heart sank. This time, though, my problem was real and I had to confront it.

While I desperately wanted to continue looking inside the fenced-off area to see why it was fenced off and to find what was there, I felt I simply didn't have any other choice; I had to get off before I was seen. Accordingly, it was four-minute-mile time. So I grabbed my camera and hightailed it back to the fence, looking back once to see if the Bedouins were following me—they weren't. I slowed up but continued making my way to the fence, then slithered through the hole I had dug in the ground and ran up to where Bob was and told him what had happened.

We decided it was best to leave, so we hopped into the truck and headed back down the road. We spent the rest of the afternoon driving in the area south of the mountain, looking for the probable site of the battle of the Amalekites. We closely scrutinized all the large rock outcroppings and rock facings along the mountain, hoping we could see more petroglyphs. We now think the absence of the petroglyphs is more significant than their presence would be had we found some more there.

The petroglyphs appear only in one place in this part of the desert—at the mountain. There are no petroglyphs, no etchings, no scratchings, no drawings to be found in any other place, nor are there boundary markers or stone monuments, nor grave sites like those we saw in close proximity to the mountain, at any place other than close to Jabal al Lawz.

About four in the afternoon we looked at each other and said, "Well, should we go have tea or not?" We decided it would be better not to. (We did not yet know how bad the tea was—had we known that, we would not even have asked the question.)

What we needed to do was regroup, get our energy and strength back. It had been a long day. Perhaps that evening we could climb up the back side of Mount Sinai. Accordingly we went south, thinking that there was a valley that would hook us around. We were unable to find such a valley, so we turned around, heading north, looking for a trail or some open space we could drive across that might lead us to where we needed to go. Eventually we found a road that seemed to go in the general direction we wanted.

Soon we were to find, though, that the road was impassable for our little truck. It went up a very steep grade and was deeply rutted. We got stuck on the high center between the ruts on our first three attempts to get up the hill. Before taking a fourth shot at it, we got out, shoveled away rocks, and tried to even a path for the tires. Finally we made it to the top and kept moving. We had come up a hill with a rise in elevation of maybe 250 feet off the valley floor which continued a general rise before it leveled off into a large, flat desert area, comprising a total of some 300 to 400 acres surrounded with jagged rock cliffs.

Camping in the Kingdom

We drove around on this flat plain, looking for a place to camp. Our requirements were simple: we wanted to be in a spot where we couldn't be seen but that also provided plenty of shade and afforded us a view of the back side of the mountain so we could create our plan of action.

We were finally able to find such a spot. We were certainly not the first ones to find it. The gully we drove into had obviously been used by many, many campers in the past. We are certain that none of them were from Montana or Colorado. These had all been Bedouin campers, which was obvious by the way they camped—they're litterbugs—and the numbers of fire rings in the area.

We again set our binoculars to the task of bringing Jabal al Lawz closer to us so we could try to pick out some way of climbing up. We decided it could be climbed from the back side. Bob was ready to make a go for it right then and there, but I wasn't.

I was worn out from my run inside the encampment and also felt we would have a better shot at it in the daytime. If something went wrong, we wouldn't have to contend with nightfall. Bob quickly saw my line of reasoning and agreed we should recoup our energy and prepare for a hike the following morning.

The first thing I did was take the shoes I had worn on my illegal trip behind the fence and hide them under a couple of large rocks. In the event we were caught, I did not want to be found with the shoes that left telltale footprints inside the encampment.

After inspection of the back of Jabal al Lawz, we pitched camp. I had a small sponge and air mattress, but Bob, with his concern about snakes, decided to sleep inside the truck. Unfortunately for him, he is taller than the truck was wide. But by propping up our suitcases and boxes of bottled water we gave him more room to place his legs outside the truck.

The weather was warm enough so we didn't need much in the way of blankets or sleeping bags. We both slept with our clothes on. Bob had a lightweight blanket wrapped around him and I opted for a Mylar space blanket, which makes for pretty good sleeping in warm weather. The problem is if there is any wind, the wind blows and rattles it so it makes a lot of noise. Fortunately, this was a wind-free night and we were quickly asleep.

That was interrupted about midnight when a pickup truck drove into our campsite, flashing bright lights on and off in my face. I didn't wake Bob up, wanting him to get as much rest as he could. I would deal with whatever the problem was. I stood up to see what this was all about and that seemed to do the trick. The truck turned around and headed back into the infinity of the desert night. Who they were and what they were doing, I will never know. My first thought, obviously, was that it had been something to do with our meetings with the Bedouins or the schoolteacher the previous day. But since they let us be, I figured we weren't the object of any great manhunt and would be able to get on with our trip in the morning.

Breakfast the following morning consisted of backpack food and a little bread.

We knew the general direction we wanted to head in to go up the mountain and knew it would not be easy. If I were by myself, I never would have attempted it, but having Bob with me was a great help. His support would help me in my moments of doubt, and mine would do the same for him.

Climbing to the Top

We left our camp at a quarter to six. As the orange sun rose over the mountains in the east, the morning cool quickly vanished. We thought if we really hustled along we could make it to the top before the extreme heat set in. We had our cameras with us, as well as a limited amount of water. We both carried small backpacks so our hands would be free, which was essential since this was more a climb than a hike. Fortunately we had the foresight to bring leather gloves with us, which were really a boon when scrambling around on the rocks.

The first half of the climb up the back of the mountain was rather pleasant. It was a nice walk up along an alluvial fan coming down from the back of a ravine. From the top of the fan, you can look out over the entire valley floor. It has that majestic sense all deserts have of seeming to stop time. We enjoyed the view at our first rest stop, then continued pushing up the mountain.

We realized we had to change our plans a little, because what appeared to be a way up the back side of Jabal al Lawz looked far too rugged. We had to strike out in a different way, and since there were no paths we just started heading up, looking for the easiest route.

About a third of the way up, there was a huge concave rock that looked to me to be a great place for people to stop for shelter—shelter from rain, if it ever rained there, but especially shelter from the sun.

We went to the rock to see what was there and found carvings and drawings similar to what we found on the front side of the mountain: people in worship of a calf or a cow. These were more like stick figures, however, and they did not show the Hathor or Apis drawing of the bull, as seen at the altar site. This was another indication to me that the altar site is really something special. At the latter, people had taken time and painstaking effort to carve out several elaborate bovine figures.

The next two hours we spent shinning up the back side of the mountain. The one thing we most wanted to do was see what accounted for the difference in color on the mountain. We had noticed earlier that from any vantage point the top of the mountain is capped in dark stones. It almost looks as though there is a permanent shadow on top of the mountain, although there are no clouds in the sky. The stones are darker and Bob was keen to head up there to see the difference between the two rocks. The first three-quarters of the way the mountain is composed of sagebrush and buff- and beige-colored rocks. It's only at the top that the mountain turns darker.

Climbing up the back side meant spreading our bodies to work around or across large outcroppings. There is no path, no trail, and frequently not even a place for a trail. The drop in many places was thirty to forty feet straight down.

By 9:15 we had crested the summit of Jabal al Lawz and stood there, sweat-drenched. We imagined ourselves as the first people, perhaps the first Christians, to ever reach this historic mountain since the time of Moses!

The view from the top of Jabal al Lawz is absolutely spectacular. You can see over the entire mountain range and almost to the Red Sea. To the north and south there is a line of rugged mountains similar to Jabal al Lawz. Looking to the east, one sees the huge valley which ultimately gives way to the desert that leads to Tabuk and to a true wilderness. It was a spectacular sight, so we sat back and enjoyed it, catching our breath and cooling off, on the highest point in this part of Saudi Arabia.

Our first objective after our rest was to gather as much of the black rock as we could for laboratory analysis. The next thing was for us to leave a note at the top of the mountain in case anyone else ever climbs up the 7,884-foot summit. If you ever get there, you will find our message, extending our greetings to whoever finds it, explaining that we would like to work to further develop this site in conjunction with the government of Saudi Arabia.

The final order of the day on top of the mountain was to take pictures of ourselves. Bob wrote an inscription in his Bible to commemorate the day.

We then headed down the mountain on the front side so we could at least have a look at the terrain below the mountain inside the fenced-off area.

We carefully picked our way along the edge of the mountain so we might get a view of the twelve pillars David had mentioned or the structures at the base of the mountain—without being seen ourselves.

What We Saw

There are some false peaks to Jabal al Lawz. At the highest point you can see that the mountain sloughs off down to the north, where another peak juts out from the mountain. There is a large plateau area between these two peaks, a kind of barrel-like indentation or amphitheater, if you will, in the mountain. We went down into that indentation to see what could be found. We did not see anything other than massive boulders well over the size of a large house strewn throughout the area. We did not find drawings or inscriptions on any of them. We wanted to continue out to the second peak, because directly below it is the cave of Elijah, but we both felt that would expose us to the Bedouins camped below. We already were concerned that we might have revealed ourselves by being on top of the mountain, even though it was early in the morning by Bedouin time.

So we gave up the idea of going to the cave, but did find a great vantage point to look down the large ravine that comes off Jabal al Lawz. Looking down that ravine, we were able to clearly see that a stream of some magnitude has come down this ravine in the past. We lay stretched out on top of flat rocks, hidden by brush, for probably forty-five minutes or an hour with our binoculars, scoping the entire valley floor.

We continually got new finds, new things to see. We would comment to each other, "Look over here, look over there, what does that look like to you?" There was much to see inside the fence and we longed to be on the valley floor instead of the top of the mountain.

By sighting off the abandoned pickup truck that spooked me so much the day before, we were able to reference the sightings. The first and most impressive was the foundation at the immediate base of the mountain that appeared to be an altar or a building of some sort, built at not quite a forty-five-degree angle with the corner peak of the building or structure facing the mountain itself. It is shaped like a boomerang except with sharp angles. We were looking down and had a very good view of it; it can be seen in some of our photographs.

We were also able to photograph a round hole or pit with numerous stones built up around it. In another distant area we could see what appeared to be a field of some sort, about the size of a soccer field, also with a rock altar of some sort at the right end of it with what might be pillars or stones stacked in a straight line. We thought these were the twelve pillars David had mentioned that could correspond with the twelve pillars of Moses.

Bob spotted an intriguing semicircle of stone. We hoped that when we got our photographs back we would have a clearer understanding of what we actually saw. In fact, when we did get our photographs back we felt less comfortable with what we had seen. Unfortunately, even with my telescopic lens, we could not accomplish as much as we would like to have. Plainly, there were objects down there for us to look at and they were man-made. That's about all we could conclude.

It was exceedingly frustrating not knowing about this site earlier, not having come here, say in 1984–85, before the government blocked the area off, stopping such an expedition as ours.

What does the government think of this site? Why did they establish it as an off-limits area and why did they do it so quickly? After all, Fasold only stumbled across this place in November 1986, and here we were in June 1988 with huge "no entry" signs. And no archaeological work was being done on the site. What could it all mean? Would a find of such Hebraic significance cause even more tension in the Middle East? Who knows?

After scrutinizing with our binoculars and photographing the area, we felt we had done everything possible, so it was time to get back down the mountain, back to our truck, continuing on to our next move for the day.

The climb down was easier on our lungs but more difficult on our legs. Going down, your center of gravity wants you to tip forward, especially when carrying a pack, so you are always leaning back, catching yourself with your legs. We got off the mountain as quickly as we could, coming almost straight down, even sliding on our rear ends—both of us tore our pants—and skipping between huge rock formations.

Our descent began at twelve and lasted approximately an hour and a half, while the ascent had taken almost three hours. With the exception of the beautiful views, we did not notice anything new coming down other than a truck in a wadi east of the area we would be traveling through. We assumed it would just be some Bedouins, so it would be "no problem."

Once we got down on the valley floor we had about a mile to go to our truck and campsite. We were walking through a wadi with some large bushes, so we couldn't see very far. We heard some voices to our left, but we just kept walking. We didn't see anything, and figured it was Bedouins yelling at their sheep.

Suddenly, though, to my immediate left there was a loud shout that sounded the way I would yell "STOP!" if I spoke Arabic.

My immediate thought was that we were now . . .

10.
At the Point of a Gun

Marching toward us were two men. One was dressed in some sort of khaki garb which we took for an army or some other military uniform. The one who seemed to be leading the way was dressed in a typical Bedouin white robe and red headscarf.

I looked at Bob and said, "It looks like our luck just ran out."

As he looked at me, the color drained from his face. We were already bushed. We had had a difficult hike. We were hot and exhausted and this was the last thing we needed: a military person carrying a rifle!

We stopped as they ordered, and began walking toward them, saying, "Marhaba," Arabic for hello, and asked if they spoke English. They did not speak English and we tried what little Arabic we knew.

They looked at us menacingly and I looked at their rifle, which was just as menacing. I was relieved to see it was a single-barrel, twelve-gauge shotgun and supposed, in the worst case, one of us would die and one of us wouldn't. It's a cumbersome weapon, especially being single shot, with a long barrel. So I deliberately stayed as close to the Bedouin as I could. Bob took the same approach. A rifle needs distance to be effective, but if you stay inches from it, the guy holding it can't get it pointed at you, and you have a chance to fight for the weapon.

Bob's concern was that these were Bedouin highwaymen who would think nothing of killing us for our expensive equipment.

We offered them food, water, candy bars, but they didn't take anything. Finally we hit upon the idea of some water. They seemed interested in that, so we gave them some, which they began drinking. There wasn't much water left in our bottle, but we told them to finish it all. In their best Bedouin hospitality, they left a few drops.

Finally, I asked the man in the khaki outfit what he did with his gun. Mimicking a bird flying through the air and shooting, going "Bang, bang, bang," I asked if he shot birds with the gun.

He laughed and smiled and nodded his head yes. Was I relieved—perhaps this wasn't a policeman or a bandit. Perhaps this was just a couple of young men out looking for some birds to shoot.

We asked if we could take their picture, and they kind of said yes, but kind of said no. I finally pulled out my VHS and did film the older Bedouin, the one carrying the gun. We chatted a little bit. He was even kind enough to put his gun down and, in fact, did not want his picture taken holding the gun.

We tried to talk to them a little bit, finally telling them we were going. We started walking away and they started walking their way. Perhaps the day was turning in our favor after all.

We walked farther down the wadi to the other side, which was a pretty good-sized hill, and were just about at our camp when Bob noticed there was an extra pickup truck there. We walked down to see our two newfound Bedouin friends going through our boxes, suitcases, and other things in our camp.

They even picked up some of our papers and were trying to read them. Fortunately, since they could not read English, they did not know they were directions to Jabal al Lawz, written by David Fasold.

I was surprised to see them probing through our personal possessions. Again, Bob and I were worried. Maybe these guys weren't so buddy-buddy after all and had been sent there for some reason.

Since we had plenty of water at the camp we offered them more. Again, they drank, taking a full liter, which they split between the two of them, quickly polishing it off. We offered first candy, then other things which we knew they would not take, and indeed, they did not.

We talked for a while. It is a difficult thing to do when neither party knows the other's language, but some of the message does get through.

They asked where we were from and we told them. Then they asked where we were going and we told them we were going to Al Bad. They asked if we were going to Tabuk. We wanted to know if they would see Ibraham Frich and gave them David's picture of Ibraham to give to him and said we had to get going. They took the picture of Ibraham, got in their truck, and drove away.

I looked at Bob saying, "Let's get out of here!"

Bob said, "You bet!"

By then I had packed up the stuff from the camp, throwing it in the back of the pickup. We jumped into the truck and hit the road.

There were three points where I envisioned trouble might be. The first would be where the road veers off to get into our secret wadi hiding spot. As we came up over the hill, we would have a good view of anyone who might be waiting for us—there wasn't anyone.

Perhaps we were out of this thing scot-free. As we went farther down the road, there was another good site by the school where someone could set up a group of cars or a block-ade of some fashion. This site, too, was clear, so by now I was pretty certain we were going to get out okay. I don't know if Bob felt that or not, because he was driving like a madman. I don't know how fast he was going because I was afraid to look. (I told him after this trip he could get a job as a cab driver in Cairo.)

The last likely point where they could stop us would be as we exited the desert floor back to the main highway, some forty-eight kilometers from the base of Jabal al Lawz, or at the gas station where we would have to gas up.

There was no one to greet us at the road, so we went to the gas station to fill up. We also had them fill our spare gasoline can, which had come in handy the day before. In fact, without it we would have run out and it certainly would have been much more difficult to start our charcoal fire that evening.

As we walked into the gasoline station to buy some fruit juice, ice cream bars, or whatever they had wet and cold, I heard the man servicing our car whistle real loud. I thought, "Uh, oh, we're in trouble now." Since one of the Bedouins had written down our license plate number (his writing paper was the palm of his hand), it could have been relayed to the police headquarters building directly in back of the Al Kan gas station.

Apparently, though, that was not the case, because all that happened was that out of the shadows a Bedouin walked into the store to help us find what we were looking for. There was no trap waiting for us inside the store. All the red alarm buttons that had gone off in this part of Saudi Arabia were in our minds. Our paranoia had certainly gotten the best of us. Behind every bush, in every wadi, we saw people waiting to capture us. Maybe it was just that we thought we stood out so much in the desert. We certainly didn't blend in, although we tried to by wearing Bedouin headpieces and light-colored shirts. We looked as much like them as possible. But then we had cameras, we had white skin, we had sunglasses, and a lot of other things that didn't fit the scenery.

We also knew that Ron Wyatt spent seventy-eight days in jail and David Fasold eight. This made us cautious.

I figured that at worst, if we did get caught, we'd be tossed in the clink for a few days, but at some point would get out. No way would we stay seventy-eight days in jail.

One thing I knew for certain is that I would never be happy until I got back inside the fenced-off area at the base of Mount Sinai. That would be a lingering thought in my mind forever—to see what's there.

After gassing up, we got out of there as quickly as we could. We took a southward turn at the junction where the road goes to Haql, where we stopped for lunch, which consisted of a can of cold baked beans and warm Pepsi. This tasted just as good as the previous day's hot grapefruit juice. I never thought hot grapefruit juice would taste good, but believe me, it is delicious—like nectar—when drunk under a relentless 106 degree sun.

Little did we know we would soon find . . .

11.
The Caves of Moses

All Good in Al Bad

There were two reasons for going to Al Bad.

The first was that if our theory was correct that Moses came up from the Straits of Tiran to Jabal al Lawz, he may well have passed through here, perhaps even setting up a camp, so to retrace his footsteps we would have to drive through this town.

More significantly, though, I noticed on an old, old map a mark indicating there were ruins at Al Bad. What types of ruins these were was not specified, but I thought it would be interesting to find out.

The drive from Jabal al Lawz to Al Bad took us through typical Arabic scenery: spectacular. There were high, dry, rugged mountains on both sides of the road. The yellowish bands of mountain are well splashed with bushes and trees and are peppered with Bedouins and sheepherders.

The only thing of any consequence on the drive from the Al Kan gas station to Al Bad was that the aches and pains from our hike were catching up with us, a muscle spasm here, a charley horse there, that type of thing, but we took it in stride. Perhaps the most upsetting thing to us was how dirty and smelly we must have been after our rough, rugged five-hour hike climbing to the top of Jabal al Lawz and coming back down.

As we got to the Al Bad area, I started looking for some type of ruins. I wasn't quite sure what to look for and I couldn't see anything. We pulled into the town of Al Bad, which probably holds 500 people. We drove about three-quarters of the way through this stretched-out Arabic version of a village, until we realized it really was a town. When it got to the point where we were running out of town, we turned around, as my map showed the ruins to be north of the town. By this time Bob had noticed something that he thought was tremendously significant.

There are a lot of palm trees and wells in the area. We had not seen such lush greenery or palm trees for I don't know how long, certainly none in the Tabuk area, none from Al Bi'r to Al Kan, none in the Jabal al Lawz area, and none on the drive down. This is the only true oasis in this region of Saudi Arabia.

Bob reminded me that at one of Moses' stops, his second, following the Red Sea crossing, there was a place with seventy palms and twelve springs. The Biblical name of this resting spot was Elim. Traditional archaeologists have identified Elim in the Sinai Peninsula and some believe it to be what's now called Wadi Gharandal. Bob and I visited this site on our first trip to Egypt, and it did not have as many palms or as much water as the town of Al Bad.

Al Bad fit the Biblical description, so we started taking photographs to show that at least we found palm trees and wells. This was evidence to fit the general scenario—suggesting that perhaps this place had been an oasis for a long time and could have been one of his camping sites. Our tired spirits were uplifted.

Amazed by what we had found, a true oasis in the middle of the desert, we continued looking for ancient ruins. We thought it was time to enlist the locals to help us. With that in mind, I walked into virtually every store on the one main commercial block in town to find someone. What I found was that it was nap time, so the town's merchants were sleeping. It's an unusual feeling to walk into, say, a tailor shop to see the owner lying on the floor sleeping. You don't bother him. Instead you walk on to the next store, which in this case was a grocery store. Again its owner or clerk was there—asleep on the floor.

I finally got up the gumption to disturb one of the sleeping merchants by saying *Marhaba*, rousing him from his slumber, and asking if he spoke English. He said no, but I could not let that stop me. I bought a couple of things from him, some pieces of fruit and two Pepsis. This was done in several stores until I reached one where I found someone who said he could speak English.

Playing it cool, I picked up a couple of lemons and put them on a scale. I said that would be good. He said, "One kilo?"

I said, "No, no, that is enough."

He said, "No, one kilo."

I guessed he sold a minimum of one kilo of lemons so I said, "Okay, one kilo," and he immediately said, "Two kilos?" I said, "No, that is plenty." I also picked up a couple more Pepsis, and thought by this time I had paid enough to get some information. I then tried to talk to this friendly Arab, in English, about old ruins somewhere in the Al Bad area. Unfortunately, he had no idea what I was talking about. All he knew was I was the best buyer of lemons and Pepsis he'd ever seen.

It quickly became apparent that his working English vocabulary consisted of "kilos" and numbers one through ten. That is all I could get out of him. Try as hard as I might I could not find any merchant who could give me assistance, so I started walking back up the street to see if Bob had had any better luck.

What We Were Told

Bob is a friendly guy and has no trouble chatting with people, even if they can't understand him, but at this moment he was talking to someone who obviously could speak English, and who was well dressed and, I imagined from his general appearance, also schooled. When I approached, Bob turned to him and said, "Please tell my friend what you just told me. He would like to hear it."

"Yes, I know the ruins you mentioned," he said. "They are just on the outskirts of town, just south of here. Those are the caves of Moses."

To say the least, I was astonished!

Here we were in the midst of the desert with someone telling us in perfectly good English that the caves of Moses were located about five kilometers from where we were standing. He was telling us in the same manner you or I might tell someone back home that the closest McDonald's was "three blocks down and two to the right."

Certainly everybody knew that Moses stayed and camped at the town of Al Bad and this gentleman was surprised that we weren't aware of it.

I asked him how he knew this and he said, "Moses was one of the Moslem prophets and it is in all their books that this was where Moses came through on his way to Mount Sinai."

I asked where he was educated. He said he was Syrian and that was where he learned to speak English. He also told us not to go into the caves. He said there was a fence around them and we shouldn't attempt to cross the barrier, since the area was heavily guarded. He went on to tell us that after camping here for a while, Moses and his followers went on to Jabal al Lawz— Mount Sinai!

Not only had we found the seventy palms, we also found a strong local tradition that Jabal al Lawz is the mountain of Moses. And Moses, according to their customs at least, had traveled on the path we were now following.

In my mind's eye we had already climbed over that fence and were inside the caves.

What a sensation. Had we nailed the biggest score of them all? Did we now have enough evidence to go public with Moses' journey? Did he, in fact, cross at our suggested Red Sea site at the Straits of Tiran, coming up on the western bank of Saudi

Arabia into the mountain Bob and I had climbed earlier that day? Was the Moslem story of the Exodus correct?

Our Syrian friend said he had to get back to work, so we shook hands, told him goodbye, and thanked him very much for his help. He apologized, saying he was running late already that day, something that apparently happens even in little towns like Al Bad.

I said "hasta luego" and also bade goodbye to one of the Bedouin shopkeepers I had purchased something from. He seemed genuinely happy that I said goodbye to him and I was surprised to hear him respond with "Bye-bye" just as in America.

Bob and I just about sprinted to our pickup. Like sharks going for the kill, we were going to go see the caves of Moses!

Beyond the Barbed Wire

We proceeded south out of Al Bad approximately two kilometers, which was exactly one kilometer farther than we had gone when we stopped to photograph the seventy palms and turned around. There on the right side of the road, two "klicks" past Al Bad, there is something that can't be missed: hills honeycombed with caves—perhaps the caves of Moses.

The caves are fenced off with a fence similar to what we encountered at Jabal al Lawz. It is about fourteen feet high with five barbed wire strands on top spaced about a foot apart.

In this compound there is a guardhouse with what appeared to be a full-time resident. We saw him come out at prayer time to face east toward Mecca, giving his afternoon prayers.

We pulled off the pavement onto a dirt road that looked like it might get us in around the back side of the fenced-off compound. We were searching for a place to go in at night to see what was in these caves. Instead of finding an easy entrance to the caves, though, we ran into an army blockade, a guardhouse, and a large gate with guards holding submachine guns, which to us was a subtle hint that perhaps this would not be a good place to take pictures or try to visit the caves. It doesn't take many submachine guns to change my mind.

We turned around, going back to the main road where we took some shots of the caves. They weren't particularly good since we were shooting directly into a bright sun, but at least we knew we had some pictures.

Exactly opposite the caves on the other side of the highway you will also see a large fenced-off compound. This one is almost six kilometers long and three and a half kilometers wide.

It is my belief that this is more likely where Jethro lived. That's what the locals told us. (Later we read a French author whose book mentions that he, too, had learned from people throughout Saudi Arabia that Al Bad is where Jethro, Moses' father-in-law, lived.) Additionally, the Syrian friend we met in Al Bad had told us that we would see on the other side of the road, opposite the caves, the old settlement of Moses. We now do believe this is where Jethro lived.

At this site, one could see many palm trees and water wells. These look like what we would call adobe houses. Maybe some of them are brick, most of them have fallen down. Clearly there are ruins here of great magnitude. There was more than an encampment here, there was some type of city. Most important, this entire area has been fenced off by the kingdom and declared a major archaeological site.

Later on that night Bob and I pondered several things. One was why the legitimate archaeologists and researchers haven't done what we had done. Why haven't they walked the path of Moses to see what they could find? What do they do? Why have they refused to accept the Bible's clearly worded statements that Mount Sinai is in Arabia? And why hasn't the kingdom gone public with these sites? They know they have something—that's why it's fenced off—but what else do they know?

Bob is as eager as I am to do things that most people wouldn't do and governments don't want done, so we discussed making a night trip into the caves. He was a little leery. So was I. In retrospect, we were wise not to go in. First of all, we didn't know if there was any writing inside the caves and if, in fact, they would be empty. Maybe all we would see is a cave with no petroglyphs. Second, with people living in the area with sub-machine guns it seemed smart not to tempt fate. However, I know I'll always wish I had been able to see the interiors of those caves.

We have talked with many people in Saudi Arabia and have tried to get a listing or a write-up of their archaeological sites, including Jabal al Lawz and these caves at Al Bad. Unfortunately, nothing has been produced by the government to tell us any more than we are telling you here.

After scouting the area we decided that there wasn't much more we could do at Al Bad, so we pushed on to Ra's ash Shaykh Humayd, which is basically the tip of land at the Straits of Tiran. Another ancient map indicated that there are ruins off this point as well, and having found the caves of Moses, we certainly wanted to see what these ruins could be all about. Perhaps there would be something that, while common for the people who lived there, would be as fascinating to us as the caves at Al Bad.

As we drove out of Al Bad heading south, Bob referred to his Bible and told me that what should happen next is that we should find a spring of bitter waters, approximately three days' travel by foot, north of the point we were going to, Ra's ash Shaykh Humayd.

The Biblical story is that after making the Red Sea crossing Moses traveled for three days without water, bringing his flock to a spring for them to drink. The water was bitter and they started complaining. Moses asked God what to do and God told him to throw a particular piece of wood into the water. He did. The water was sweetened. The Israelites drank and rejoiced.

We checked our odometer readings to see how far we had traveled, knowing how far it was to Ra's ash Shaykh Humayd. We started looking at kilometer reading seventy to see if we could locate a spring along the road. Nothing appeared.

The Springs of Marah?

However, at the seventy-fifth kilometer reading, we started to see a large, dry, alkaline lake bed off to the right, or west, side of the road. There were several old, dry lake beds there. Some were sizable, some about the area of a small fishing pond. A couple of them were smaller than that. In any event, they looked like alkaline water pads where water had come down and collected during the years.

We pulled our trusty Datsun off the main road and started bouncing around on dirt and sand roads once again, to drive to this area to see what was there. We took photographs so you can judge for yourself. Are these the bitter springs referred to in the Bible?

These dry, alkaline flats certainly look like they could produce bitter water and are large enough to have supplied water for Moses and the tribes. They look similar to the dry, alkaline flats that you see in my native state of Montana, where indeed the water would be very bitter.

We had learned a couple of interesting things at Al Bad. We thought we had a pretty good feel for about how many people were traveling with Moses, judging from the size of the caves and the buildings. It would appear that there must have been at least 50,000 people (and most likely a great many more), based on the size and number of buildings and the area the kingdom has fenced off.

So when we were looking for the area of bitter water, we knew it couldn't be just a small spring. It had to be water of some size. There we were, approximately three days by foot north of our proposed Red Sea crossing site. There was obviously a large amount of water in this area, most likely in the springtime, keeping in mind we were here in June, way past the wet season.

Our photographs clearly show the old alkaline lake beds, and more interestingly show where people even to this day dig for water. You can see in the photograph a tree in the background, which is unusual, because there are not a lot of trees in this area. So here we have a dry, alkaline lake bed with an occasional tree around it, which would provide the wood for Moses to toss into the lake; you can also see where people are still digging holes to pull up water. Please note the groove on the side of the hole, which has been dug about eight feet into the ground, where a water bucket on a rope has been pulled up.

Obviously we do not know if this area is the long-lost springs of Marah. But the circumstances fit: the size, the distance, and the alkalinity.

We had decided to go to Ra's ash Shaykh Humayd so we could follow the entire passage of Moses. On our earlier adventure in February, when we had gone down the Egyptian peninsula to the crossing site, we fondly looked across into Saudi Arabia, wondering if we would ever get there. Bob and I felt that we had perhaps become the first people to ever totally follow the footsteps of Moses—going from Egypt into the Red Sea at the Straits of Tiran, out onto the Arabian shores, and up to our proposed mountain.

Ra's ash Shaykh Humayd would be our campsite that night. There is a mosque there that doubles as a small military installation. Also in that area one should find a substantial number of ruins as indicated from one of our older maps. We wanted to see these ruins.

We drove down to the beach to see if we could find a camping spot, but all we saw were signs in Arabic which appeared to say: "Don't camp here," "Don't park here." Accordingly, we drove back to the mosque and, in our best Arabic, asked if we could go for a swim and camp on the beach for the night.

The bottom line was: yes, they would allow us to camp on the beach if we would give them our passports to hold for the evening.

We did want a place to camp; we wanted to get clean. We wanted to dive into the ocean and scrub off the dirt and stench. We were leery about giving up our passports, however. After all, who knows what they would do. Maybe they would make a quick check and find out our entry papers were not quite what they purported to be. Or maybe they would have some other reason not to return them. Who knows, they might even lose them. But we figured any group of people that prayed so many times a day couldn't be too bad. Besides, we doubted if the communication system was good enough to run the necessary checks, so after clowning around with them for a little bit, we left our passports and headed for the absolute tip of the Straits of Tiran to spend the night.

The first thing we did upon arriving at the beach was to change into our swimming trunks and wade out into the Red Sea. At this spot the water was very shallow—we went out about 400 feet, yet the water never touched our waists. We both dove into the water, rinsing our hair with ocean water, replacing one form of dirt for another I'm certain. But we were glad to take the alternative. We were both wearing thongs, as we did not want to step on any sea urchins or coral.

We played around in the water for a while. I warned Bob to look out for jellyfish. I knew he had a real fear of snakes but didn't know if he had a water fear or not. As a gag I pinched him on the back of his leg.

Suddenly he turned to me and shouted, "Watch out, there's a lionfish! Get out quick!" I didn't know what a lionfish was but I knew by the way he said it he wasn't kidding. I wasn't going to stand around to argue or ask what a lionfish was. So I, too, started swimming as fast as I could to get out of the area. Of course, wearing sandals you don't swim too fast. I swam about twenty feet, took off my sandals, and kept swimming, as I noticed Bob was making like a torpedo headed for shore. There were literally wakes on both sides of him.

This guy was moving. I knew he could swim but I didn't know he could swim *that* fast. Finally he stopped and I dog-paddled up to him.

He then told me about lionfish. They are one of the most poisonous fish in the ocean—large and puffy with tentacles that extend out from the entire body. At the end of these tentacles are sharp, barbed hooks the lionfish uses to inject its victim with a venom that paralyzes and stuns most anything, including humans. While the lionfish is not aggressive, just bumping up against one has been known to be fatal.

Shaken, but a little cleaner and much refreshed, we waded back to the shore and pitched our camp. For dinner that night we had more of our backpacking food and drank a tremendous amount of water. We were both dehydrated from the heat and the climb up the mountain. After dinner we sat back, a little in awe of what we felt we had established that day.

Going from the top of the mountain that perhaps Moses also climbed, then down all the way to where he probably emerged from the sea was quite an experience. The feeling was heightened when we considered that along the way people had told us, "Yes, Moses has been here." Gazing into the campfire, we meditated on the caves of Moses, as well as his original settlement—that was quite a way for us to end the night. Our only concern was that there would be nighttime marauders on the beach.

Here are the notes from my diary on that day; they may give a better sense of what we were feeling:

9:36 P.M. Sunday, July 11, 1988

In our minds, we have documented and established that Moses did cross the Red Sea, where he crossed it, where he camped along the way on his trip to Mount Sinai, where Mount Sinai is, where the golden calf was constructed and later demolished by Moses. I need to add before I forget it, as it is dark and I am tired, that we now think the large stone monuments we saw yesterday (that we thought were burial sites) probably were the boundary markers the Bible refers to when it says that Moses was instructed by God that no one should go up on the mountain except Moses.

God told him that the rest of the people, even the priests, should stay outside or they surely would die. Those markers, from our vantage point from the top of the mountain, seemed now to not be burial areas, but markers, as they formed a pattern or line in their construction. So we are of the opinion they are boundary markers.

I feel a real sense of completion tonight: as I prepare my

bed in the back of our Datsun pickup, I can look across into Egypt to see the lighthouse at Râs Muhammad, a point where earlier this year we had been held captive by the Egyptian government in our quarantine or house arrest and now here we are going to sleep on the Saudi side! It's the place people told us we would never visit. Looking across, feeling we have unlocked the mystery of Moses' travels, I want to read the Koran to learn what it says about Moses. It will be interesting to see what it says about the crossing and what documents or evidence in those writings will help us further establish our discovery.

There are two monuments of the present day in front of us. When I look to my right, I can see lights above the mosque beaming down upon the waters. I don't know if these are for military purposes or to warn ships. When I look out the tailgate of the truck I see a hill about fifty yards away, and fifty yards higher a pillbox. We will visit that tomorrow morning. It is most likely a remnant of the 1967 Sinai War. Maybe thousands of years from now people will come back looking for signs of our culture, only to find this pillbox. It is a real sensation to be inside one of them and peer out. You can hear the sounds of war, feel the crawling of death inside these structures.

Note: It is warmer this evening at sea level than it was at the 3,000-foot elevation where we were last night. This is a sultry evening. The salt air seems to penetrate everything. I am sleeping in a T-shirt (I could never have done that last night) with my space blanket wrapped around me.

Bob has been in a good deal of pain. He slipped a disk, pulled a muscle, or did something in his lower back and has taken some powerful medicine to ease it. He was in a lot of pain today as well as under a lot pressure to get up the mountain, but did it. That's a real tribute to him because it is a difficult enough mountain to climb when you are not in pain, let alone when not all of your muscles are functioning correctly.

Anywhere else in the world, the campsite we have tonight, with the ocean on both sides of us, a spectacular view, warm salty water (if you don't count lionfish), would sell for $300 to $400 a night, and here we have it all for free. That is, if we get our passports back in the morning.

When I awoke in the morning, Bob said we had had visitors at night shining spotlights on us. I hadn't noticed, I must have been really out. As the sun rose over Ra's ash Shaykh Humayd, we started the day with oranges and bananas. I reflected on power brunches at the Plaza in New York City, and the best brunch I've ever had, on Easter Sunday at the Del Monte Lodge in Pebble Beach, California. Neither of those matched the sheer joy of our breakfast that morning in Saudi Arabia.

In spite of the previous evening's swim, we were still pretty grungy, so we decided to shampoo our hair to get the saltwater out before going to reclaim our passports. We must have been a colorful sight there on the beach, heads covered with soap-suds. It was certainly the most unusual shampoo I've ever had, but it also felt better than any other. We started the day clean. Under those layers of dirt, both Bob and I found a lot of sun-burn, especially on our noses. The rest of our bodies had seemed to acquire a pretty good tan, even though the sun is so unforgiving. Bob noticed he was sunburned on his wrist where the holes from his watchband were.

On the Road Again

After packing up we headed to the mosque to see how our luck would fare for the day. We walked around to what we took to be the front where a guard with machine gun was stationed. We were given a warm greeting by the soldier with the gun, who was one of the fellows we had clowned around with the previous evening. It looked like things were going to go smoothly. We asked for our passports and chatted a little bit while someone went to get them.

We told them we were doctors. They asked about our skills and seemed to get a kick out of our pantomiming the profession by showing how one would use a stethoscope or peering down another's throat. That really brought the house down.

We got our passports back, said a thousand *shokrun*s (Arabic thank you's), and shook hands with everyone in sight. It didn't matter if they were carrying guns or not, whether they were operating radios, or simply staring at us, we shook everybody's hand hoping to make them feel good about us—especially about our getting out of there.

Incidentally, this does seem to be the best thing to do in Saudi Arabia. If someone approaches you, stick out your hand and shake theirs. Try to do it before they do. You'll find they almost always beat you to it. Whether they are arresting you, as we found out later on, or whether they are willing to beat you up, as we heard from others, the first thing they want to do is shake your hand. It is kind of a nice custom and nice feeling to actually walk up to a total stranger with your hand extended. It certainly is a sign of friendship and bridges the communication gap.

As we were walking away from the mosque, I looked again at our campsite, which was absolutely stunning right on the bay of the ocean. It was so beautiful, I asked if I could take a picture.

Asking that question was about like walking into a police station and saying, "Do you want to buy some drugs from me?"

The guards immediately said, "No, no, no." Then they asked if we had cameras and if we had taken pictures. Of course all of this was in some sort of sign language, mixed Arabic and English.

We immediately said no and showed we had no cameras on us. Bob went back into his doctor routine, putting an imaginary stethoscope to a man's heart, checking his tongue and pulse. It drew a little laughter, but not nearly as much as the first time.

We assured them we had not taken any pictures, which was partly true. We hadn't taken any that morning, but we did get some nice photos the previous evening at our campsite.

Apparently they were afraid we were going to take pictures of their military installation, which amounts to a couple of guards with machine guns protecting a large radio tower on the bay and the pillbox we found by our encampment. It could be that this type of military hardware would be significant and would indeed be valuable information to some government somewhere, but I could hardly imagine that this military mosque installation was important to anybody's security.

Eventually we were able to extricate ourselves from this situation by showering them with more *shokrun*s and assuring them we didn't have cameras. We moved as quickly as we could to the truck without alarming them, popped in, and headed north, getting back on the main paved road toward Al Bad. What a relief it was to be in our truck with our passports—and our cameras—with about twenty rolls of exposed film in hand.

We had to watch the odometer to note when we had gone thirty-four kilometers, which would be where the springs of Marah are. When we got there we went off the paved road and drove onto the alkaline flats to see more closely what was there. We had noticed several things the day before—large mounds of dirt scattered throughout the dry lake beds. I wasn't certain whether these were burial markers or tombs or just what they were, but upon closer inspection we were able to see they were mounds of dirt left over from the holes people had dug in the wet season to gather water.

Most experts have said essentially that despite the many locations proposed as the site of Marah, none has gained the complete confidence of scholars. Later, we were to find one source that describes the springs as "unpalatable bitter pools of water reached by the Israelites after they crossed the Red Sea and entered the Wilderness of Shur." Notice the reference here is not to just one body of water or spring, but to pools—which certainly conforms to the area we found.

Our primary point that morning was to rephotograph the caves with the sun at our back instead of our faces. So we made fast time back to Al Bad where we carefully photographed the caves.

Not Alone

As we were doing that, a car stopped about forty feet away. We heard a whispering voice telling us in English to stop taking photographs and to come over to the car.

We did so, only to meet a Scot who works out of the Philippines in Saudi Arabia. He is an engineer for a communications company there, and confirmed what we'd heard the previous day: he also said that these are the caves of Moses. In fact, he said all of his Saudi friends referred to these as the caves of Moses, or perhaps where Jethro, Moses' father-in-law, lived. He told us that one of the caves is the cave where Moses' wife lived with his father-in-law. Based on the opinions of archaeologists we have since talked with, however, we think that these caves were not homes but burial caves.

Although he was surreptitiously taking photographs himself, he warned us not to be seen with cameras in the area.

At 9:06 on that Monday morning we exchanged cards with our new Scottish friend, with the promise to communicate what we had found there. We also told him a little bit about Jabal al Lawz, so it was fair exchange. We got into the truck and headed back to Tabuk, feeling we had come, we had seen, and perhaps we had conquered.

It was time to leave Saudi Arabia. It was time not only to leave the kingdom but, more important, it was time to see if we could get out of the country what we had found in the country. So far, no one had been able to do that.

We would next be faced with . . .

12.
Leaving the Kingdom

On the way back toward Tabuk, I started to get the sense that the trip was over prematurely. That was not a good feeling. Instead of heading straight to Tabuk and home, my preference would have been to have Bob drop me off late at night, about two or three in the morning, so I could sneak inside the wire fence to see what was there.

I figured after the first break of dawn I would have the sites picked out that I would want to photograph. I'd shoot pictures (a roll of color and a roll of black-and-white) and get out to meet Bob at some safe place down the road. I couldn't imagine the Bedouins being awake at that hour. And if they were, what would they do?

They have no phones, no CB radios. All they could do is physically detain me, but Bob would be free to go and do whatever needed to be done. They wouldn't know about him, only me. I also had a pretty strong feeling I could outrun any of the Bedouins. First of all, they wear sandals and I had on nice hiking-jogging boots. Second, I'm a runner, and most likely am in much better shape than they are. I'm sure I could go a lot farther.

Of course, they have trucks and could follow us. But in the remote areas of the mountains, I felt I stood a pretty good chance even if my penetration of the fenced-off area was noticed. If pursued, I would have to ditch my camera and just keep the film. It would work.

We felt in our heart of hearts that Moses did come into Saudi Arabia, but I wanted more documentation. We found what could be the cave of Elijah. We found Al Bad, where it appears Moses camped, the caves of Moses, and the seventy palms. We found Jabal al Lawz, photographed it. It appears to meet the conditions of Mount Sinai. We found the petroglyphs, with an indication that perhaps that is where the golden calf was worshiped.

I asked myself, though, Would this evidence hold up in a court of law, let alone with a major publishing house? Bob argued that we had enough evidence; I felt we needed more pictures. We had come so far and it had taken so much money and time that it seemed one more trip back to Jabal al Lawz would be worth it.

I reckoned that if we threw in the towel at this point, we would most likely never be back. And second, it would be back to civilization, back to the humdrum existence of trading commodities, back to riding on airplanes, not trucks, back to sleeping in our own beds, not isolated beaches.

But Bob felt otherwise. He felt we had to get back, and he wanted to be back in Colorado. Besides, we had ripped loose a shock absorber on our now rattling pickup and probably wouldn't make it back to the mountain anyway.

Yet several glaring questions remained to be answered. Some of those I felt Bob had not yet asked himself, but suspected that he would after leaving the desert. It seemed too easy to accept everything at face value because it fit the facts we wanted to see. Strong convictions can blind one to analysis of all the facts and cause one to wrap those facts around one's beliefs to make them fit.

I did not want that to happen with this project. It was too thrilling and too big to botch up, only to have some university professor throw sand on it later. But Bob prevailed and we kept driving, past the turnoff to Jabal al Lawz, and headed the Datsun back to Tabuk where we checked in at the Sahara, cleaned up, got some decent food, and made reservations to be homeward bound early the following morning.

The Difficulty of Getting Out

I thought the excitement and surprises would be finished, but checking out of Saudi Arabia was more of a problem than I had anticipated it would be. *Leaving* Saudi Arabia is similar to *entering* most countries. All in all, there were seven passport checks on our way out. There were four luggage checks. Our luggage contained some things that it shouldn't (notably rocks and film) but nothing that they would probably notice. However, Bob did get flagged in Jedda for the Rambo-style scabbard knife in his suitcase, which he usually wore strapped to his left leg.

I was questioned about some of the rocks from the top of Mount Sinai. The luggage, with the exception of the photographs we had taken, really did not indicate much to security.

What concerned us most was that since we had not been in contact with "our man in London," we had no idea if our visas were still valid, or if the phony fax copies had been discovered.

The most harrowing moment came in Jedda when we were checking into the international terminal. There you have to fill out a card telling what you were doing in Saudi Arabia, where you went, who your sponsor was. Bob and I had forgotten the exact name of our sponsor so we did the best we could from memory. We were a little bit nervous about that. In fact, Bob was thinking about going through without writing the sponsor's name down, but after observing people in line ahead of us, we saw that I had made the unfortunate error of filling mine out in red ink instead of black. So when I got to the head of the line my card was ripped up and I was told to do it over again in black ink. (Since then, I have deliberately used red ink in other countries and have not been rejected.) That's not unsettling if you are traveling on valid visas, but we weren't, so that was strike one.

Strike two was the line to have our papers checked. Bob and I seem to be blessed with Murphy's Law when it comes to standing in line. Whatever line Bob or I get into is going to be the longest and slowest. Leaving Saudi Arabia certainly was no exception to that rule. The reason our line slowed up was there was a new fellow on duty who was being trained, and he had to do it absolutely by the book since the supervisor was with him. Bob spent more than five minutes with him, whereas everyone else spent less than one minute.

I finally saw Bob walk around the corner and that was the last I was to see of him for almost an hour. By the time I got my papers checked, the supervisor was all over the trainee. And he inspected my papers as if he were an eagle looking for spawning salmon.

The fact that my passport had expired and had been reissued caught their attention. They wanted to know how long ago it had been reissued, so I told them—it was right there on the passport. They then asked why I was going to New York and I said I was going back earlier than I thought because I had a daughter who lived there, and then to Los Angeles. They said, "But your ticket says you were going to London." I said, yes, we had changed our plans. That caused a little bit of commotion and they started accessing their computer files to see what they could find out about me.

I couldn't read what was on the computer terminal because it was in Arabic, obviously a great advantage for them. They next pressed a few more buttons, looked at my visa exit card, and asked what I had been doing in Jedda, asked why I didn't go to Riyadh. I gave them the best explanation I could think of. Of course, it did not include Jabal al Lawz.

Finally, I heard one of the most comforting sounds possible: that of a hand stamping your visa documents. So there was to be no strike three. Part of me wanted to run, jump up in the air, and click my heels together, but I thought that might not be acceptable, given the circumstances. So I walked slowly, deliberately, only to see that there were yet two more checkpoints ahead of me, one for luggage, one for airline tickets, but they were not much of a problem.

I finally found Bob, who did not have as much of a problem as I had. All that was left to do now was to wait for our plane to take off, about three hours.

Questioning Our Actions

On board the jet, we started tabulating what we had done wrong to see if, in fact, the trip could have gone better. In that analysis we think that, first of all, entering the country without legal visas was wrong. While, in fact, we did not falsify the documents ourselves, we certainly knew of their suspect credibility, and that was an error.

Second, we had entered restricted areas when I bolted the fence at the Mount Sinai site. This offense may not have been quite as severe as illegal entry, but considering the jail time Fasold and Wyatt had done, we decided that, on reflection, there might be a better way to do all this.

The pictures we took of Moses' cave were clearly illegal and should not have been taken—but how else could we establish such things? After the local townspeople told us, "Yes, those are the caves where Moses stayed, those are the caves Moses' father-in-law lived in, this is the area Moses lived in and came back through on his trip to Mount Sinai," how could we walk away, so all we could do is tell about it and not have the photographic evidence?

We had to get the pictures and we did, and we felt that was the right thing to do. Then, of course, there are the pictures of the ruins of Mount Sinai. Those also should not have been taken because that area, like Moses' cave, is blocked off by the government. That goes for the petroglyphs as well, which is probably the single greatest bit of evidence to establish Jabal al Lawz as Mount Sinai. We fractured some of the laws of the kingdom in getting the pictures, but there wasn't any other course to take. After all, if you go three-quarters of the way around the world and feel you may have made a major archaeological find, you want to take back more than just some entertaining yarns.

Did we get anything in return for all this? You bet we did. We got pictures of petroglyphs of what appears to be the golden calf. We have clear photographs of what certainly appears to be the altar where the golden calf was worshiped and was most likely burned by Moses. We have photographs of what we think are the boundary markers around the Mount Sinai area (as commanded by God to keep people off the mountain). We found grave sites. We found the ruins of the temple. We photographed around the twelve pillars.

We have photos of a semicircle of smaller pillars. And, of course, we reached the top of Mount Sinai and photographed more petroglyphs (that no one, to our knowledge, has ever talked about) on the back side of Mount Sinai. We also got the photographs and the testimony on Moses' cave area in Al Bad.

We located the well site where, most likely, Moses encountered bitter water approximately three days from the Red Sea crossing site. We certainly made a clear and direct hit with the seventy palms. And earlier in the year, we had found the Red Sea bridge.

All of which fit nicely with the timing of Moses' journey from Egypt into Saudi Arabia.

Oh sure, there is more we should have done and more I'd like to do. I would like to climb back into the cave that we dubbed the cave of Elijah (on the mountain to the north of Mount Sinai) to see what, if any, petroglyphs are in there, to see how large the cave is.

We should also have gotten more ground-level shots of the area at the base of Mount Sinai. But we reached the conclusion, and I think it was a wise one, that we had maybe 90 percent of what we needed—we had the facts. We had the photographs. With more covert activities, we increased the chance of getting apprehended and losing everything we had gotten. (Like on a late-night trip to Las Vegas, where you have been gambling for seven or eight hours and are well ahead; you keep thinking: when is the house going to catch up with me? You know they will.) After three days in the desert of the real Mount Sinai, it was time for things to stop going our way and start going the other, so, in retrospect, it was probably a good time for us to split.

Our mission had been accomplished; we had done what no one else had done since the time of Moses. In our minds, we followed the exact footsteps of the Exodus—from Egypt, down its eastern side, to the real Red Sea crossing at the Straits of Tiran, then from the Saudi Arabian side of the Straits, on up to Jabal al Lawz, the real Mount Sinai.

Was it worth the risks and expense? Absolutely. And I can only say, dear reader, if you ever get the opportunity for this type of adventure—take it. If nothing else you will have some great stories to tell your grandchildren.

Bob and I certainly operated at different levels on this trip. Bob from Scripture, I from logic. It all seemed very logical, almost elementary, to track the footsteps of Moses. What I find astonishing is that researchers have not done what we did. Why have they been so willing to accept places that don't fit, in any way whatsoever, with the Biblical description?

For Bob, I think, the trip adds more fuel to the fire of his religious faith and that's a nice thing to see happen. I did not have a religious experience or change of ideas or convictions. I still have my view of the way the world works, what God is and what God is not. How following the footsteps of Moses fits into this is something that I will have to wait and see.

I felt like a hunter. We had bagged game, maybe one of the biggest of them all. In any event, whether we came back empty-handed, or found nothing but rejection of our ideas about Mount Sinai, Bob and I, for the rest of the our lives, will have a vivid memory of a fascinating experience only a handful of people would be willing to have.

We were out of the kingdom, we were safe, and we had a great story. We also had . . .

13.
A Second Thought

Bob and I returned home with good feelings. We had accomplished what we set out to do.

The first thing we did was to make mad dashes to film developers to see if our cameras had captured what we thought we saw. We were anxious to share these pictures with others to get their impressions.

Reality began to set in when we started showing our slides and photographs to our friends. While they enjoyed our story, we could tell they were kind enough to stretch their imagination to envision what we had seen. We could tell, looking into their eyes, that they were still more than a little skeptical about our story, that our evidence was not totally persuasive.

Bob got slightly better reactions from his friends in the religious community than I got from my friends and neighbors. Obviously, they wanted to believe us, but there was that look, not only because of the immensity of the project but because on close inspection the photographs do not show clearly enough or exactly enough what we had seen.

Bob and I talked over the phone, wishing we had taken a larger telescopic lens with us. But the fact is we hadn't, and we had not come home with enough evidence to knock the socks off anyone looking at our photos or listening to our theories.

Going Back?

So what could we do? I think the answer was obvious. We had no choice. We had to go back. We had to enter the kingdom again to get more conclusive evidence of what is at the base of Jabal al Lawz.

It was imperative, to my way of thinking, that we have photographs of the twelve pillars that David Fasold had mentioned to us, which are compelling evidence linking the Bible to this particular mountain.

After all, can you envision any other mountain, anyplace in the world, having twelve pillars at its base? And what would that mean? Wouldn't it most likely mean that if you found a mountain, any mountain, in the general area of where the Exodus is to have taken place and it had twelve substantial pillars at its base, that it would be an excellent candidate for the title of the real Mount Sinai? What are the odds of twelve pillars, plus everything else we'd found scattered at the base, being at any other mountain?

We also wanted to get closer to the V-shaped altar site at the base of the mountain to see what that structure was like. And we wanted to enter the cave of Elijah.

The local Bedouins had told us there were many wonderful and unique drawings in the cave. And we know from David's research that there is gold in or about the cave, perhaps jewelry the Israelites took from the Egyptians. Who knows? But without getting inside it, we wouldn't know. That was for sure.

Accordingly, we decided to make a trip back. This time we thought we would be on a little safer ground since we knew the terrain and knew exactly what we wanted to do and the best way to do it. While our harrowing journeys make for good copy and lots of humor, there is a more important side to what took place. That is the purpose of this chapter, to tell you the results of our second entry.

Indiana Jones?

Some people wonder if we are not trying to live out the life of Harrison Ford as Indiana Jones. That's not true. We have noticed there is a glaring discrepancy between what happens to us and what happens to Indiana Jones. Believe me, the discrepancy is not a little one. There are really two discrepancies between what we do and what Indiana Jones does. First of all, Indiana Jones apparently has no problem getting through customs. And he always gets the girl.

On our return visit to the kingdom we expected to have no problems getting in. After all, we had our visas from our first trip. But upon checking into Saudi Air once we got to London, we were told our visas were no longer good, that they were only for a single entry. There we were. Stuck in London again without visas to get into the kingdom. Bob and I looked at each other not knowing whether to cry or laugh. We decided it would be better to laugh and call our good friend Dimitrie.

We gave Dimitrie's office a call, only to find that our dear friend was out of London. My next call was to a better friend, Jack, to see if he could be of any assistance. He said, "Sure, no problem. Come on over and we'll get you through."

Two days later we were still in London. Jack was pulling strings and calling in markers, but we were still sitting on our rear ends, waiting. We were on better ground this time, though, because Jack was working on real papers to get us into the country, not phony faxed papers.

Jack was a good host to us, inviting us to his apartment to watch the Tyson-Spinks fight, which, though good, was terribly short-lived. The fight was shown in London about 3:30 A.M. and we were to get our papers and be on our plane by eleven the same morning. After the fight, we had a bite to eat, cleaned up a bit, and started to prepare for the day, getting everything packed so all we had to do was grab our stuff, pick up our papers, and be on our way.

Bob had the foresight to get hold of Peter, the cab driver, who had helped us so much on our first entry to the kingdom. He told Peter we would give him fifty quid if he could get us through the maze of bureaucracy at the Saudi embassy again.

Peter was more than willing to oblige, taking us to the embassy and going inside with Bob. Bob turned over our passports and papers to Peter, who then went around back to see his friend. I waited outside, watching a line of almost 150 people who had queued up in front of the embassy, seeking, in their fashion, to get inside the kingdom. Truly, we had been blessed to find Peter.

About forty-five minutes later, Bob came sauntering down the embassy steps flashing the thumbs-up sign. This time we would be in more legally than the last time.

We hopped in the cab, and Peter shot off like a rocket. This was almost a replay of our first trip, since we had about forty-five minutes to make an hour-and-fifteen-minute drive to the airport. Peter continued his Steve McQueen impression, weaving, bobbing, and ducking in and out of London traffic.

This time when we presented our passports at the check-in along with our visas, we were simply told to proceed. We checked in our luggage and went down to the holding room to wait for boarding of the flight to Riyadh.

The next leg of the journey was pretty much a mirror image of our first trip, except everything was less eventful, from the flight to Jedda to checking into the hotel and renting a truck.

Since we knew where we were going, we did not have to ask as many questions as we did the first time and could do things much more on our own, so we quickly got our supplies and headed out to Jabal al Lawz.

This time we had no problem finding the turnoff from the Al Kan gas station and we knew where to find that will-o'-the-wisp path that some people claim to be a road. We made the correct turn and traveled the dusty ruts to the mountain.

We arrived about 3:00 P.M. and took a few photographs, Bob

got more photos of the petroglyphs, and we drove down to where we think the battle of the Amalekites most likely took place. We also were able to stand on what we have determined to possibly be the boundary markers set out by Moses. In so doing, you can see how they encircled the base of the mountain with the purpose of keeping everyone away from the mountain, as was commanded.

Starting Our Nighttime Entry

We then found a campsite where we could pitch our stuff and proceeded to work out our plan.

Our plan was simple, thanks to the aid of our infrared nightscope. I'd picked up the scope in London, and we were pleased to have it with us. We knew it would be a real advantage for what we had planned—a nighttime foray into the fenced-off area at the base of the mountain.

We had come a long way, physically and psychologically, to make this penetration. But it could not be done during the daytime. Thus, we had only one alternative: to go in at night along the lines of our original scenario, find what we wanted to photograph, wait till daybreak to take our pictures, and leave. We chose this trip to coincide with the full moon to give us as much light as possible.

Both Bob and I were more than a little nervous. We knew the risks of what we were doing this time around. While our entry papers were more legitimate than last time, we had no entry papers for the fenced-off area and there would be no excuse if we were caught there.

We had scouted the area during the day and had found that things had changed quite a bit. Our initial expectation was that we could drive down the old road where I had found the petroglyphs, park our truck behind some rocks, and cross the fence about where I had the first time.

This had to be ruled out, because now a Bedouin sheepherder had pitched his camp atop the road. There must have been four or five tents, several hundred sheep, and numerous people running around.

We also found what appeared to be sentries on the north and south extremities of the mountain site. We camped north of one of these, about half a mile on the other side of the valley floor, out of his view, back behind some large rock outcroppings.

The best way would be to walk behind the guards, which meant we would have to do a good deal of climbing that we had not expected. We would have to travel north from the valley floor, across the floor, and then climb back into the hills and up some small peaks to place ourselves out of the sentry's range of sight.

We tried to get some sleep because we were both tired from the trip, as well as the late Tyson-Spinks fight the previous night. But this was to no avail. We simply couldn't sleep, so we decided to make it appear someone was sleeping in our camp. We set up air mattresses, put blankets on top of them, then stuffed the blankets with clothes and bushes to make it look as if people were sleeping there. To the casual observer it would appear that two guys decided to sleep on the valley floor for the night.

In fact, though, those two guys had left the area. And by midnight, our trek to the mountain had begun.

Getting Past the Guards

With the aid of the infrared scope we were able to pick our way across the valley floor, going one person at a time in spurts of about fifty yards. One of us would crawl in places and hunch down in others to get a vantage point to see what was happening. That person would have the nightscope; the next one of us would then catch up. We played this form of hopscotch across the valley floor, looking out for Bedouins and sentries.

There were dogs to the north of us that apparently picked up our scent, as they began barking. We feared a sudden attack by these ferocious sheepdogs protecting their flocks from predators. There was nothing we could do about that, however. We had no choice but to press on. Eventually, we were able to cross the valley floor and work our way up a ravine. Once we did that the dogs stopped barking.

From the ravine, we did not exactly have a clear idea where we should head, but we knew we had to go up higher and south. So that's what we began doing, picking our way along the wadis, hoping we would not stumble across some encamped Bedouin.

After about forty-five minutes of slow, tedious night travel (we were going as slowly as possible, because we did not want to make noise or disturb people who might be camped out; we had no idea if anyone was there or not, but we certainly didn't want to surprise them), we thought we were almost directly behind where the sentry truck was parked. To check on that, Bob crawled over to the edge of the wadi, looked down, and sure enough there it was. A glowing cigarette ember told Bob someone was inside smoking and most likely unaware of our presence. So Bob made his way back to where I was and we continued on with our journey up the wadi, constantly gaining higher elevation.

We crossed numerous old Bedouin camps that night. Each one of them made our hearts pound, because we weren't certain if there were people still in them or not. We had to first look very closely at the camp with our nightscope. If it appeared no one was there, one of us would quietly go into the area. Once we confirmed it was safe, the other would follow. That continued to be our pattern for the next hour until we reached a point where we thought we would be significantly behind the fence—somewhere in the area where David had told us we would find the twelve pillars.

Searching for the Twelve Pillars

In actuality we had climbed so high and so far south that we were about halfway in the midst of the fenced-off area. We then had a choice. We could head farther south to the absolute base of the mountain where the V-shaped foundation or temple site was that we noted from our first trip, or we could head back to the area where we thought the twelve pillars were.

We finally decided to head back to where the twelve pillars were, and with the aid of moonlight and the scope were able to make our way there.

Since there was a guardhouse inside the fenced-off area we were extraordinarily cautious and moved as silently as possible. Everything was done in whispers and hand signs. (We didn't talk out loud to one another until the next morning.) David told us we would find that he had dug into one of the pillars. His descriptions of the pillars were that they were eighteen feet in diameter, spaced five feet apart. The pillars are constructed in a wall-like fashion with three rings of stone. We risked taking two flash photos as we were a mere fifty yards from the guardhouse; unfortunately, our nightime shots did not come out well so I have done a drawing of what these look like.

David and Wyatt had dug down into one of the pillars about ten feet. As the pillars apparently had been covered by a mud slide or something in the ensuing years, they are embedded in the ground.

We climbed a vantage point above the guardhouse to see if we could find the dig David had mentioned and also to check out the guardhouse to see if anyone was on duty that night. We could not tell, though, since no lights were on in the shack.

We were able to finally locate what looked like the pillar site and decided to make our way down to see what was there. A curious thing happened on our descent. While we could see the area of the pillars, as we got down to the area we couldn't find them—not at all. Bob and I both thought we had made pretty good cross sightings of what would zero us into the area, but once down on the valley floor, we couldn't find the pillars.

After a furtive thirty-minute search we finally crawled over to each other and whispered we had no choice but to climb back up the hill to get another bearing as to where they were.

So that's what we did. Back up the hill, being careful not to make any noise. Again, we sighted the one dug-out pillar with the aid of the nightscope and carefully picked our way down over rocks and cactus one more time to see if we could locate it. This time our luck was better, but it still took us a long time of crawling on our bellies and hunched walking in and out of shadows behind rocks.

Once we found them, frankly, they were not as impressive as I had hoped. But I guess that's the way it is with archaeological things. People like Moses don't leave neon signs saying they were there.

We were able to inspect the pillar site, though, and could see that, in fact, Fasold's description was accurate and correct. The walls of the pillar are comprised of rocks, the outside perimeter made of rocks ten inches in diameter, and this wall parallels the inside wall. There is a larger, squarish rock placed between the outside and the inside rock perimeters, giving a total look to the wall of about two and a half feet.

We could see where David and his crew had dug; in fact, to about ten to twelve feet. We risked taking a couple of photographs, hoping that no Bedouin or sentry would be out for a midnight stroll.

Unfortunately, the roll of film with these pictures on it is one that we had to toss out on the desert. Nonetheless, both Bob and I will attest to seeing the pillar and that it is approximately eighteen and one-half feet in diameter. There were other pillars on both sides but we did not have the time or ability to uncover all twelve pillars as he had.

Here is the way David described the pillars as he saw them in daylight:

> We saw these circles and we started scraping the dirt off with our feet. We could only describe them by saying they were like brick. Let's say that the outer circle is eighteen feet in diameter and let's visualize it as bricks that were laid

in eighteen-foot-diameter circles end to end. Then what we'll do is move in and make another circle inside the outer circle about sixteen feet in diameter and lay those end to end. Now, in the space in between those two circles, we'll take bricks and lay them side by side all around the area between the two circles. That will give you an idea how these stones are laid. The stones are not dressed.

It was a fifteen-foot-diameter circle in the center. We dug a pretty deep hole. We had to get a tree branch, which was not easy to find around there. We got some kind of old tree branch and put that down in the hole. That's how they would get in and out. That's how deep we dug the hole. But we didn't dig the hole fifteen feet in diameter. What we maybe should have done is dug alongside, rather than right in the middle and we could have followed the stone down to see just how deep those pillars were. There is a possibility the pillars go down only a foot or two.

We found twelve of these circles, eighteen feet in diameter, and spaced five feet apart, very symmetrical. Four of the circles are on a magnetic bearing of 193 degrees.

Pillars five through twelve started to curve along the bank of the wadi, near that mountain that looks like it might be Sinai (the one all dark on top) that's bearing off to the right 260 degrees.

I don't think they would go to that much trouble to make a campsite with this many stones. Bedouin tents are not circular like an American tepee. I think it is probably more like a freestanding tower.

Standing on ring number four, there is a line of rings closing off the triangular area where the temple is.

We did not see any other rings in the area. It was difficult to take a picture of them. We had tools, we had about eight construction workers from Samran and two Toyota jeeps and an archaeologist.

The archaeologist was more concerned with the Apis and the Hathor carved on the rocks.

It looks like there was a landslide on the mountain, which spilled into the wadi and covered the pillars.

I think the archaeologist was aware someone was poking around there before, perhaps his name was Orange. He had thought something up there was of importance. I mentioned to him that some of the stones from the temple area were dressed real nice, but we're told they were removed in the 1930s to a place in Haql, by truck I presume, and used as building blocks for a mosque. So my idea was always to go up to Haql and see how much of this stone was in the mosque and get an idea how big the temple was.

There was mention that the temple was put there by Sulliman, I think the name could have been Solomon.

When I said to Ebraham [a local Bedouin], "I want to walk to the mountain of Jabal al Lawz," he said, "Jabal moussa henna"—"Moses' mountain is here." When I told that to Ron he asked the Bedouin if there was anything of interest to see around here and he said there were remains of an old temple.

Ron ran up the hill, fell, and gashed his leg.

The archaeologist said the cow inscriptions on the rocks were definitely Egyptian. Egyptian ruminations of Apis and Hathor. We made the connection that this is where they worshiped the golden calf.

You could see where if Moses were coming down from that mountain he could see across the wadi where the petroglyphs are, and that he might come down and inquire what's going on across the wadi.

David asserts that when he was caught at the site by the local authorities, the government men went down the shaft he had dug in the pillar and appeared to remove some objects—probably the gold he'd been digging for. Unfortunately, they would not disclose what they'd brought up.

After we had documented and photographed the twelve-pillar site, we decided it was time to move on to the temple site.

Looking across the hills and valleys, we realized it would be a good half-hour walk toward the pillar site and we would be exposed much of the time in bright moonlight. But it was one of those situations when you don't have much choice. We simply took our time, moving in and out of the shadows as much as possible, making no fast moves, gently gliding along, shadows in the night.

The terrain is very rocky and ragged, which made the going even more arduous. Had we been able to see, we still would have had difficulty. There is a road that meanders through this area, but unfortunately we did not cross it until we got about 200 yards from the altar site.

The altar was back in the moon shadow of the mountain, so it was perfectly dark. We felt relieved that no one would be able to see us as long as no one was right there. Since we had not encountered any sheep or dogs, we felt comfortable for the first time that night that we were on our own.

Finding the Pillar Stones

We got about thirty yards away from what we call the temple or altar site, and noticed there were pillars along the side of the road. These pillars were eighteen and a half inches in diameter and twenty-two to twenty-four inches tall. They appear to be columns. One could almost describe them as being marble columns. They are not fluted columns. They are smooth, but definitely hand-chiseled.

You have already read what David had to say about them and their use. What struck us was the anomaly of finding this type of material so far removed from civilization. It would be comparable to finding marble pillars in the middle of the Mojave Desert. Things like that just don't happen. They get there for very specific reasons, and it must be a reason of consequence and significance for people to have developed this type of structure.

We had not realized on our previous trip, looking down on the altar site, what the white flecks on our photographs were, but now we knew. They were indeed pillar stones. We risked taking another photograph, which shows Bob standing on top of one of these pillar stones at the base of the mountain. This picture was taken about 3:00 A.M.

212

Inspecting the Temple Altar Site

We proceeded then to the temple site and took its measurements, which are twenty-one and a half inches in diameter by eighteen to thirty inches in height. The interesting thing about this altar site is that it appears to be a foundation of some sort—almost like a rock formation you could build something on top of. Yet there is no appearance of its being used as a foundation. While it has the outer walls of a foundation, there is also a parallel wall inside the foundation itself, equally as high. I estimate the walls of the foundation to be three and a half feet high and eighteen to twenty-four inches in width.

Inside the foundation there is another row of rocks that runs parallel to the outside walls. It remains a question to us just exactly what the structure was used for. The significant points we noted are that the structure is not made of cut rocks and is not polished rock. These are local rocks that have been carefully stacked and fitted into this unique configuration, a wedge, that points directly up the draw to the tip of Jabal al Lawz.

We do know that for thousands of years Bedouins have roamed the valley floors of this region. Yet at no place in our travel, nor in any literature, have we heard or read reports of stone buildings or foundations being found in this part of the world, which makes this find even more fascinating.

In addition, there were those smooth pillar stones most of which apparently have now been removed and used to build a mosque in Haql. What we found was the aberration of a stone structure in the midst of a desert that is not known for stone structures. The Bedouins, for thousands of years, have slept under tents, as their nomadic existence precludes permanent building sites.

After poking and prodding around the altar area for about ten minutes, I moved farther up the canyon to see what the circular sites we had spotted from the top of the mountain were. They were difficult to locate because of the roughness of the terrain and the darkness of the night. But with the aid of the nightscope I was able to make them out. They appear to be circular rings of some sort, around which perhaps people sat, or still do, to talk. It is difficult to say. They are about twelve feet in diameter and are definitely man-made but I was not able to ascertain their purpose.

The Ascent to Elijah's Cave

Finally Bob and I agreed it was time to start thinking about getting out, but we thought before we did that we should try to get to the cave of Elijah.

Thus began our ascent to the cave at about 3:30 in the morning. It was still dark but thanks to the moonlight we could see where the cave was on the mountain and started making our climb. This was indeed a climb, probably the most treacherous I have been on in my life—treacherous not only because there was plenty of slough rock and talus, but because it was all climbing hand over foot. There were no trails, it was a scramble up a rock cliff. But of more consequence was the fact that it was dark and we were unable to use the scope. The scope was good for viewing and observing things in the distance but on an up-close basis it was of little value.

We tried to haul ourselves up over the cliffs, picking what looked like, with what light we had, the most logical way.

About halfway up the mountain, Bob fell, careening off the rocks. He landed on the ledge where I was standing. I grabbed on to him and he caught his balance. That was lucky, because it was a fifty- to sixty-foot straight drop below us. That caused us to pause and reconsider what we were doing. We decided to go on, but take it slower and be more careful.

The farther we got, the lighter it also became, so we were starting to get benefit of daybreak. But by the same token, we would soon be seen. We had to get to the cave of Elijah shortly or we would be totally exposed on the face of the mountain.

We had chosen to wear drab clothing that night because it looks black in darkness and in early-morning light it would still blend in with the rocks. But soon our pitch-black clothes would stand out against the white rocks.

We also reached a point where we both realized we were not going to be able to get to the cave. We could see it, and we desperately wanted to be there, but our light was not good enough to allow us to see the best way to get there. It was getting more treacherous, steeper, and we had long since drunk all our water. We were worried about being spotted, so we decided about 300 yards short of the cave that we'd better turn around or we were going to be in for trouble.

We considered having one of us go to the cave and spend the entire day there, with the other going back that night. We decided it was best for the two of us to stay together. Down the mountain we went.

Coming Down

It felt good to start working with gravity as opposed to working against it, as the climb was hard and intense. We were both perspiring like crazy and had a long way to go. We could see we were next going to be dodging daylight.

In fact, by the time we got down to a safer area on the mountain, we began circumventing the mountain instead of going straight down. Daylight had clearly broken. We could see the Bedouin camp across the valley. We only hoped they could not see us. We hoped they were sleeping to their hearts' content, with visions of sugarplums dancing in their heads.

We moved as fast as we could around the face of the mountain, trying to get to a draw where we could hide and continue our journey back to the truck.

This took probably twenty-five minutes, and during that time we were completely exposed. Apparently we were not seen and we got to the draw where we stopped, hid behind some rocks, caught our breath, looked at each other somewhat playfully, and gave a sigh of relief. We said to one another, "Well, we've done it again!"

The rest of the hike back to the truck was uneventful. We were able to stay in a large draw which blocked us from the sentry at the north of the mountain, as well as from the Bedouin campsite and the guardhouse. Nobody could see us and we could see nobody as we skirted around the fence. That was exactly the way we wanted it.

The only thing we would have to deal with was walking across the valley floor, where we would again be totally exposed. But we did not feel that would represent a problem, even if someone accosted us out there. We could say we were out for a morning stroll, leaving out where the stroll took us.

We gingerly picked our way across the valley floor as quickly as we could, threw everything in the truck, and opened up bottle after bottle of water, drinking in huge gulps. We both completely drenched our shirts with water as it ran off our chins. It was now full daylight and it was a splendid morning, with the sun spreading its warm rays across the desert.

We thought the next thing we wanted to study was where the battle of the Amalekites may have taken place, so we decided to head south of the mountain to the large plain area we had seen on our first trip.

The plain opens itself up to a huge mesa about a mile and a half south of the mountain, and that's where we went. Along the way we looked for markings, stone structures, and so forth, but were not able to find anything other than the sheepherders' rings they place on hillsides.

As we entered the large plain area, we saw it was massive. It is probably fifteen to twenty miles long and seven to ten miles in width. There are several large promontories sticking up on it. One of these could well have been the hill Moses sat upon during the battle with the Amalekites.

The Bad Times Begin

We then headed farther south hoping to find some type of old road that would take us to the town of Al Bad. That was our undoing—another thing that happened to us that doesn't happen to Indiana Jones: he never gets lost—we did.

We got totally turned around. Even with our compasses and maps, we were flat-out lost. The best solution we could see was to try to pick our way out of the valley, which we tried. But that only got us entwined deeper in the mess. Accordingly, our next thought was to ask one of those "friendly Bedouins" for assistance. That was our undoing, as you can read about in the first chapter of this book. By asking for help, we were eventually led to exactly where we did not want to go—jail.

Let me recapitulate what we think we accomplished on this particular mission.

First of all, we documented that the pillars are indeed there. We saw them, we touched them, we photographed them. We did the same thing with the altar site. We also documented the smooth pillar cut stones at the altar site which appear to have been from another time period, and for the most part have been removed to make a mosque in Haql.

In light of what the Bible says should be at the mountain—twelve pillars, altar site, worship site for the golden calf, among others—it all adds up to something.

What is that something?

It seems to us that all the evidence fits in with Biblical description. Therefore, we have constructed a bridge of faith saying that since all the facts fit the description, this is most likely the true site of Mount Sinai. Indeed, it may not be, but if that's the case, then whatever did occur at this mountain is unique and unusual, and it needs to be investigated by professional archaeologists.

Sure, Bob and I would like to be part of that adventure, but it doesn't have to be done with us. The point is, it does need to be done.

Someone must cross over and beyond our bridge of faith and establish the truth of this site, to know beyond a doubt what did take place here—why all of these significant elements would converge around this mountain—and to tell us, once and for all, that this is indeed the Mountain of Moses.

Epilogue

In the fall of 1989 I hired George Stevens of Horizon Research to pull infrared photographs from the French satellite system and to analyze the various color spectrums to see what he could tell us about our proposed Red Sea crossing site and Jabal al Lawz.

The use of infrared photographs in archaeology is just now coming of age—or into vogue. Several major sites have been discovered using this technique. It works by capturing the differences in heat patterns on the surface of the earth.

For example, a trail through a jungle will be hotter than the surrounding jungle, and sophisticated films and filters can now be used to isolate and track these minute and otherwise undetectable variations in heat intensity.

Or, if a building were dismantled and the foundation removed or covered up with dirt and left to stand for a hundred years or more, no longer visible to the naked eye, infrared photography would clearly show the outline of the building. Even slight ground disturbance can be detected and recorded many, many years after the fact.

George worked with these techniques in the military. From his headquarters in Searchlight, Nevada, he now uses them to help in mineral exploration. (On rare occasions, he's been known to leave the mundane hunt for gold and silver veins to assist those of us in search of more consequential objects!)

The Exodus, By George

As the book was going to press, George called me with the results of his analysis of the infrared photographs:

"First, there is a clear trail that comes into the photograph from the left side. It is south of the traditional Mount Sinai and goes right to the water's edge at the Straits of Tiran, at the Gulf of Aqaba."

I had given George the latitude and longitude of the Red Sea crossing site, as well as those of Jabal al Lawz. That was his target area. His report to me was based on a study of that specific spot, and it sounded like a bull's-eye.

"It is a very clear trail and very, very old," he continued. "How old?" I asked. He told me,

"It is impossible to tell the exact age from the photographs, but it is certainly thousands of years. That's for sure.

"It was used heavily, and has some real width to it at parts. [This fits with the 600,000 in biblical reference.] There are some very large campsites along the way, on the other side of the straits, where it seems to come out of the Red Sea."

I interrupted, "Wait now, George. Do you mean to tell me, the trail goes to the Jackson Reef area and then starts all over on the other side of the Red Sea . . . in Saudi Arabia?"

"Yes, that's what happens—the trail goes right down to the straits and resumes on the other side. It runs south for a way, from where it begins in Saudi Arabia, then turns north, paralleling the Red Sea."

Needless to say, he had my full attention. But I wanted to know how all this could be detected. How did he know?

George (who I know is not a student of the Bible, and if pushed would probably say he's a nonbeliever, that he is simply a scientist) explained to me that by using special filters on the negatives, one can detect different colors and densities of colors. Although specifics are obviously subject to interpretation, to the trained eye—as his was in military service for many years—certain patterns of prior activity are quite apparent.

I asked more about the trail, and George continued.

"It goes about eleven miles south of the crossing site, then turns up north. There are three major campsites, or areas

220

where there were towns or gatherings of many people. I can't tell you what went on there, only that there were large congregations of people. Finally the trail turns east, about halfway up the gulf [that's where the caves of Moses are—something I never told George about], and heads inland, going right to the area you marked on your map as representing Jabal al Lawz. There is a huge, well-used campsite there.

"I doubt if you could see much, if any, of the trail if you were there, but the path is very apparent from the photographs. From the mountain you are so interested in, it just disperses. It does not continue on in any one direction."

To me, this sounds like the Exodus trail, the path so many have sought so long. It is, to my mind, the final piece of evidence to substantiate this mountain, Jabal al Lawz, as the Mountain of Moses, to which Moses took the twelve tribes and upon which he met face-to-face with God. What else could it be, given what we found on the site, the Biblical description, and now the evidence of today's most high-tech space photography?

As a final check, I asked George to tell me what he saw around St. Catherine's, the other area for which I had him pull photos. In the event the traditionalists were right and I was wrong, I had to know.

"There are several pathways around that mountain, but no major camping sites. And based on my study and interpretation of the density of the colors in the photographs, I'd say the trails there are no more than three hundred to four hundred years old, at the most. The trails there don't even come close to the size and apparent age of the one that goes into and out of the Red Sea."

It has been quite a journey—from Egypt, to diving the depths of the Red Sea, to Saudi Arabia, to the caves of Moses and on to Jabal al Lawz.

I hope you have enjoyed our caravan and gained a few new insights into the Bible—the Exodus in particular. I truly believe that previous searches for Mount Sinai *must* have found that the physical evidence did not fit the Biblical story, so conjecture was used, assumptions made, and premises reached which would later be disproved.

My greatest joy from the adventure is not in finding what we sincerely believe is the true Mountain of Moses, but in knowing that the evidence we did find makes the Bible once again our most accurate source for what took place those thousands of years ago. From our view on the ground, or the satellite's view from space, what the Bible says about the Exodus is real and provable. Everything is as it should be.

And Now . . .

Dateline August 1990. Out of the ancient port city of Ashkelon, Israel, report of the recent discovery of a small bronze statue of a calf, which many are saying is a style of art that could be representative of the golden calf of Exodus fame. The find, the work of a team of archaeologists from Harvard, has been preliminarily dated to around 1550 b.c., a date consistent with what many scholars feel represents the time of Moses' journey to Mount Sinai.

From photographs we are able to see several similarities with the drawings we found at Jabal al Lawz. No more than 6 inches long, the statue has three distinct body parts: head, body, and legs, a demarcation existing also in the petroglyphs. As lines separated the body parts in the petroglyphs, so different materials seem to have been used in the small sculpture.

Perhaps more significant, though, is that the overall body configurations are similar in both. The body is elongated, with the head out of proportion to the body of an actual calf or bull; the horns are not prominent in either representation, and the belly lines of both seem similar in style.

This consistency of style could be vitally important. The congruency between the two artifacts simply adds credence to our theory—one more grain of evidence to place upon the scales in the continuing saga of Mount Sinai.

Bibliography

The Amplified Bible. Grand Rapids: Zondervan, 1965.

Asimov, Isaac. *Asimov's Guide to the Bible.* New York: Avon, 1968.

Batto, B. *The Reed Sea: Requiescat in Peace.*

Burckhardt, J. L. *Travels in Syria and the Holy Land.* New York:AMS Pr., 1983.

Cassuto, Umberto. *A Commentary on the Book of Exodus.* Jerusalem, 1967.

Encyclopedia Brittanica. 9th ed.

Flavius, Josephus. *The Antiquities of the Jews.* Jerusalem, 1960.

Forster, Charles. *The Historical Geography of Arabia.* Vol. 2. London: Darf, 1984.

Har-El, Manashe. *The Sinai Journeys.* Los Angeles: Ridgefield, 1983.

Harper's Bible Commentary, ed. James L. Mays. New York: Harper & Row, 1988.

Harper's Bible Dictionary, ed. Paul J. Achtemeier. New York: Harper & Row, 1985.

The Holy Bible, Revised Standard Version. Minneapolis: Augsburg, 1952.

The Holy Bible, Revised Standard Version. New York: Thomas Nelson, 1952.

Keller, Werner. *The Bible As History.* New York: Bantam, 1974.

Koenig, Jean. *Le Site de Al-Jaw Dans l'ancien Pays de Madin.* Paris, 1982.

Palmer, E. H. *The Desert of the Exodus.* New York: Harper Brothers, 1872.

Petrie, W. M. F. *Researches in Sinai.* London: Murray, 1906.

Shanks, Hershel, ed. *Ancient Israel.* Washington, D.C.: Biblical Archaeology Society, 1988.

Smith, William. *Smith's Bible Dictionary.* New York: Jove, 1977.

Taylor, William. *Moses, The Law Giver.* New York: Harper Brothers, 1879.

For more information on developments in the authentication of Jabal al Lawz as the true Mount Sinai, or for speaking engagements, please contact Larry Williams, Box 8162, Rancho Santa Fe, California, 92067. Tel.: 619-259-6748